Brain Ticklers in Nature

Published by :
Lotus Press Publishers & Distributors

Brain Ticklers in Nature

Maya Badri

Lotus Press

4735/22, Prakash Deep Building
Ansari Road, Darya Ganj,
New Delhi - 110002

Lotus Press : Publishers & Distributors
Unit No. 220, 2nd Floor, 4735/22, Prakash Deep Building,
Ansari Road, Darya Ganj, New Delhi- 110002
Ph.: 23280047, 98118-38000
• E-mail : lotuspress1984@gmail.com
www.lotuspress.co.in

Brain Ticklers in Nature

ISBN: 81-89093-72-X

Printed & Published by : **Lotus Press Publisher & Distributors,** New Delhi-02

PREFACE

Quiz time is a popular pastime with children in India today. With television and its myriad channels playing host to several quiz competitions, there is no dearth of quizzers in our country today.

This book is loaded with interesting facts about nature in a question-and-answer format. There is an interesting mix of animal and plant life, ecology, geography and evolution patterns.

Nature with all its beauty must be enjoyed. I hope you will find this nature quiz just as appealing and interesting as the marvels of nature.

Maya Badri

CONTENTS

1
BLOOMS AND BLOSSOMS

Given below are a few interesting flowers, but sadly the letters are all jumbled up. Unscramble them to discover the beautiful flowers.

1. a a a i c c

Clue: a flowering shrub with round white or yellow flower clusters.

2. a e e n m n o

Clue: small wild or garden plant with white, red or purple star-shaped flowers.

3. a h i m n t u u r

Clue: showy, richly coloured flowers cultivated in greenhouses.

4. a h i i m n r r t u n

Clue: type of garden flower with bag-shaped petals which open when pressed.

5. a e r s t

Clue: daisy-like flower with a yellow centre, and white, pink or purple petals.

6. a c e h h n m m r y s u t

Clue: white, golden or garnet in colour.

7. a a h i l d

Clue: cultivated for its showy, large, variously coloured flower.

8. a d i y s

Clue: a small white flower with a yellow centre, usually growing wild.

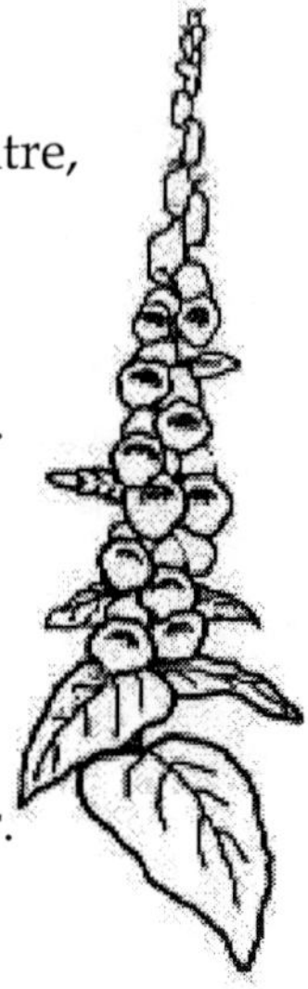

9. d e i l h m p u n

Clue: a plant with tall spikes of blue flowers.

10. e f g l o o v x

Clue: purple or white bell-shaped flower.

11. e e f a i r s

Clue: a fragrant yellow, pink or white flower.

12. a d g i l o u s l

Clue: spikes of bright coloured flowers in pure white, deep yellow, vivid orange or scarlet, pink or purple.

13. a h h c i n t y

Clue: a sweet-smelling bell-shaped flower growing from a bulb.

14. a c i l l

Clue: a sweet-smelling pale purple or white blossom.

15. e i l n p u

Clue: a talk spike of flowers, bearing seeds in pods.

16. a g i l m d r o

Clue: a white or orange flower.

17. c d h i r o

Clue: a brightly-coloured flower, with one petal larger than the other two.

18. e n p o y

Clue: a large, round pink, red or white flower.

19. h l o p x

Clue: a cluster of reddish, purple or white flowers.

20. i l p t u

Clue: a large, brightly-coloured cup-shaped flower on a tall stem.

21. a b e e g r r

Clue: an electric-hued, daisy-like flower.

22. a n p y s

Clue: broad, flat, brightly-colour petalled flower

23. a a c i n n o t r

Clue: sweet-smelling white, pink or red flower.

24. c h h l l k o o y

Clue: tall plant with brightly-coloured flowers.

25. b e c p t t u u r

Clue: bright yellow cup-shaped flower.

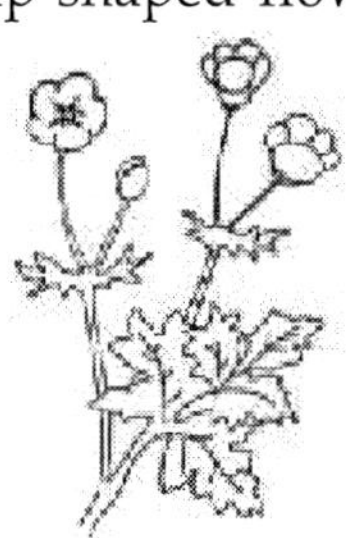

2
SAY IT WITH FLOWERS

Answer 'True' or 'False'.

1. The floating *Wolffia angasta* from the duckweed family are the smallest flowering plants.
2. Cleistogamous flowers remain closed and never open.
3. The dahlia originated in Mexico.
4. England began growing tulips about three hundred years ago.
5. Raphaelesia, the world's biggest flower, grows in Austria.
6. The trumpet-shaped flower, resting amongst broad heart-shaped leaves of a climbing vine, is called a moonflower.
7. The garden plant with orange, red or yellow flowers and umbrella-shaped leaves is called gladiolus.
8. The flower *Kniphofia* is better known as the red hot poker.
9. The agapanthus is a vigorous bulbous plant.
10. The perennial phlox does not need much space to grow.
11. Cyclamen has a short period of flowering.
12. Bougainvilleas are evergreen plants.
13. *Helipterum roseum* is commonly known as paper daisy.

14. Zinnia is named after the botanist, Dr. J.G. Zinn.

15. The common red rose is also called the Mistress of the Night.

16. The *Crocus sativus* is the plant whose flower yields the saffron of commerce.

17. *Brosimum utile* is the national flower of South Africa.

18. The white flowers which flourish on hemlock plant produce an unpleasant smell.

19. The world's largest rosebush is located in Tombstone, Arizona.

20. Honeysuckles have red and white flowers.

21. Poppy is a poisonous plant.

22. The orchid takes it name from a Greek word meaning 'testicle'.

23. The bottlebrush flowers are known for their small stamens.

24. Saffron is obtained from poppies.

25. Nicotania is a kind of lily.

Rose

Poppy

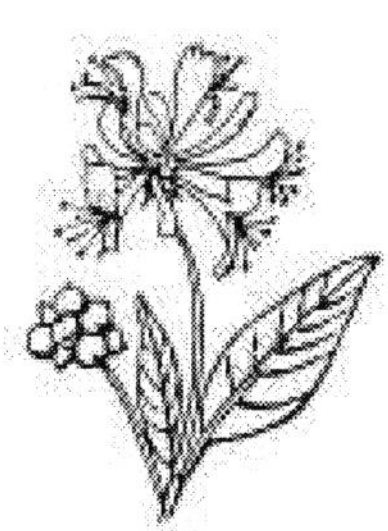

Honeysuckle

3
FLOWERY EMBLEMS

Listed below are the names of flowers which are emblems of the various states in America. Match them with their states.

Flower	State
1. Saguaro cactus	a. Alabama
2. Indian paintbrush	b. Arizona
3. Western rhododendron	c. Arkansas
4. Red clover	d. Texas
5. Sego lily	e. Ohio
6. Bluebonnet	f. Vermont
7. Camellia	g. Wyoming
8. Iris	h. New York
9. Apple blossom	i. Minnesota
10. Mountain laurel	j. Utah
11. Scarlet carnation	k. Washington
12. Purple violet	l. Nevada
13. Rose	m. Pennsylvania
14. Sagebrush	n. New Jersey
15. Lady's slipper	o. Tennessee
16. Magnolia	p. Iowa

17. Wild rose q. Indiana

18. Orange blossom r. Massachusetts

19. Peony s. Florida

20. Mayflower t. Louisiana

4
A GARDEN OF FLOWERS

Given below are names of flowers, but they are incomplete. Fill in the blanks with the appropriate letters.

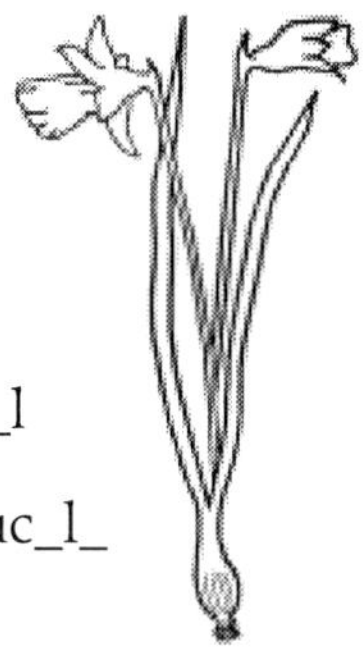

1. Az_l_ _
2. B_ls_m
3. C_sm_s
4. D_ _f_d_l
5. H_n_y_uc_l_
6. B_g_n_ _
7. Hi_is_u_
8. Ca_ _a
9. C_r_sa_t_em_m
10. V_ _l_t
11. Co_ _f_o_er
12. S_ap_ra_on
13. P_t_ _ia

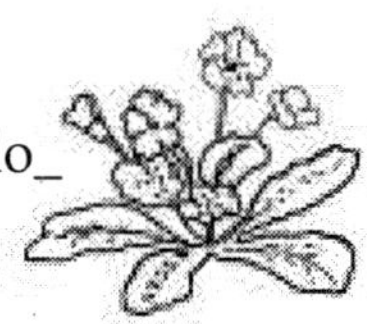

14. S_ee_p_a
15. L_r_s_ur
16. Su_ _lo_er
17. P_ _ny
18. P_n_y
19. C_ _n_ _io_
20. P_im_o_e
21. B_t_e_ _up
22. D_i_y
23. C_oc_s
24. Sn_ _d_ _p
25. G_ _ani_ _m

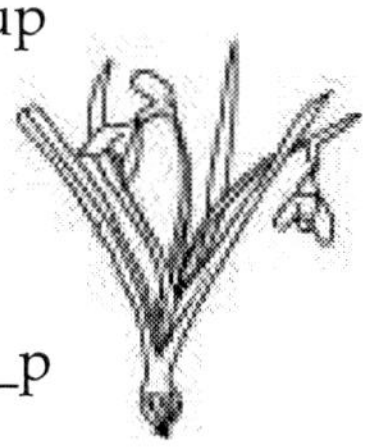

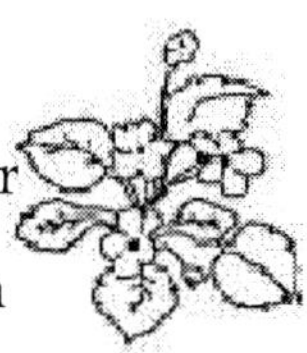

5
WHAT FLOWER AM I?

Given below are clues to certain flowers. Guess the flowers.

1. I have strong-smelling, yellow flowers. I am easily propagated by my large black seeds. I provide long-lasting cut flowers. In Mexico, I am known as the 'flower of death'. And an ancient legend says that I am the flower that the Virgin Mary wore to symbolise the warm glow that radiated around her head. Do you know what I am?

    a. Marigold ☐

    b. Narcissus ☐

    c. Goldenrod ☐

2. I am a tender bulb with dramatic flowers, originally from the Andes mountains of Chile and Peru. My name, translated from the Greek, means 'sparkling', and I am named after a shepherdess in Greek mythology. I am flower from late fall to early spring. I am quite popular as a Christmas gift.

    a. Amaryllis ☐

    b. Lily ☐

    c. Orchid ☐

3. I have over 500 species, but for the most part, I am a vine that thrives in warm climates. Once I get going, I can really take over your garden. My seeds are highly toxic. But don't let that scare you away! I can add beauty to any garden with my wide variety of flowers and colours. My

name is something that you might say to wake up a child or a loved one.

a. Morning Glory ☐

b. Sweet Pea ☐

c. Honeysuckle ☐

4. I can grow up, over and around nearly anything that lies in my path. In fact, Robert Frost, in his famous poem, "The Woodpile", "wound strings round and round it like a bundle". But I also have beautiful, abundant flowers that make me a stunning addition to any garden. And with more than 200 species, I can grow pretty much all over the world.

a. Honeysuckle ☐

b. Climatis ☐

c. Morning Glory ☐

6
QUALITY FLOWERS

Most flowers denote human qualities. Match the flowers with their qualities.

A	B
1. Azalea	1. I love
2. Bachelor's Buttons	2. changeable
3. Begonia	3. sincerity
4. Camelias (red)	4. unpretentious excellence
5. Carnations (white)	5. purity

6. Chrysanthemum (red)
7. Cyclamen
8. Daffodil
9. Dahlia
10. Daisy
11. Forget-me-not
12. Gladiolus
13. Hibiscus
14. Iris
15. Lily (white)
16. Narcissus
17. Nasturtium
18. Orchid
19. Pansy
20. Peony
21. Raninculus
22. Rhododendron
23. Roses (red)
24. Snapdragon
25. Tulip
26. Violet
27. Zinnia

6. regard
7. sporting
8. constant love
9. consideration
10. temperance
11. radiant charm
12. loyalty
13. jealousy
14. bashfulness
15. rare beauty
16. sweet and lovely
17. innocence
18. celibacy
19. true love
20. diffidence
21. bravery
22. communication
23. refinement
24. caution
25. ego
26. thoughtful recollections
27. danger

28. Sweet William	28. modesty
29. Hyacinth	29. fame
30. French Marigold	30. presumption

7
HANDSOME FOLIAGE

Answer 'True' or 'False'.

1. Tea leaves contain an alkaloid called caffeine.
2. A medicine called Atropine is prepared from the leaves of *Atropa belladona.*
3. Cocaine is prepared from *Papaver somniferum.*
4. The leaves of the pitcher plant contain an acidic enzyme.
5. The sundew plant has hair-like structures on the upper surface of the leaves.
6. In the Venus's Flytrap plant, the two flaps of the leaf start folding like a book when touched.
7. Deciduous trees shed their leaves every year.
8. When leaves become weak and fall from trees, the process is called defoliation.
9. Photosynthesis occurs only in green plants.
10. The fern tree stems have tips which bear palm-shaped leaves.

11. Fern leaves are used to prepare mattresses.

12. The leaves of a raffia palm can reach up to 65 feet in length.

13. During midsummer, the radical leaves of the compass plant invariably point precisely east and west.

14. Cacti have leaves.

15. In the walking fern, the leaf tips develop into new plants if they touch the ground.

16. The cabbage stores food in its leaves.

17. The pine is made up of compound leaves.

18. Bamboo leaves are narrow and long.

19. Onion leaves are thin and long.

20. The giant leaf of the water lily of South America can be up to 1.8 metres long.

21. The teak tree has broad leaves.

22. The leaf is born from a stem.

23. Pollinating insects are lured by certain bright-coloured leaves.

24. The rubber plant leaf blades are smooth-edged.

25. Mosses are full of leaves.

Papaver somniferum

Fern

8
NUTCRACKERS

What are these nuts? Fill in the blanks to find out.

1. _ l _ o n d

2. B _ _ e l _ u t

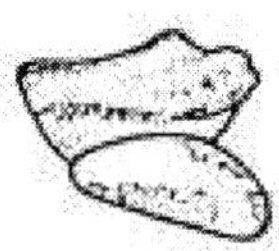

3. B _ a _ i l n _ _

4. C _ s _ e _
5. C _ _ o n _ t
6. A _ o _ n
7. P _ _ t a _ _ i o
8. K o _ _ n u _
9. N _ t _ e g
10. P _ c a _

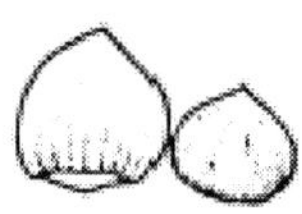

11. H _ z _ _ n _ t

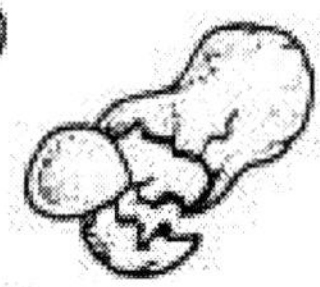

12. P _ _ n u _
13. C h _ _ t n _ _

14. W _ l _ _ t

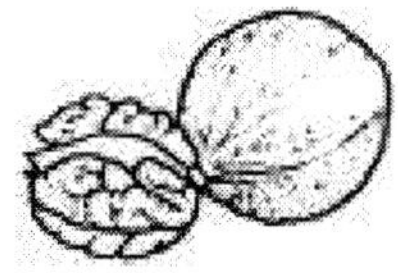

15. A _ e _ a n u _
16. H _ c _ o _ y

9
FRUITY FLAVOURS

Name these fruits.

1. A round fruit with firm juicy flesh, and red, green or yellow skin when ripe.
2. A large, juicy tropical fruit with sweet yellow flesh and a prickly skin.
3. A sweet, juicy, yellow or green fruit with a rounded shape that becomes narrower towards the stalk.
4. A round, thick-skinned juicy fruit that is a reddish-yellow colour, and related to the tangerine.
5. A long, thick-skinned edible fruit that is yellow or green when ripe.
6. A round fruit like a lemon, but smaller and more acidic.
7. An oval, yellow fruit with acidic juice used for drinks and flavouring.
8. A green or purple berry growing in clusters on vines, used for making wine or eaten as fruit.
9. A soft, round, smooth-skinned dark red or maroon fruit with sweet flesh and a flattish pointed stone.
10. A round or oblong green or orange edible fruit with small round, black seeds in it.
11. A pear-shaped green fruit with flesh which is yellow or orange when ripe, and the skin too turns orange. It has a large seed inside, and is a tropical fruit.

12. A very small fruit with a sweetish white pulp and a single seed in a thin brown shell.

13. A round stone-fruit with soft flesh, related to the plum and peach, and orange-yellow when ripe.

14. A round, juicy fruit with downy yellowish-red skin and a rough stone. People love to have such a complexion!

15. A small, bitter, oval fruit, green when unripe, and black when ripe.

16. A large, juicy, round fruit of various types of plant that trail along the ground.

17. A thick-skinned, round fruit which, when ripe, has a reddish centre full of small juicy seeds that are edible.

18. A tropical fruit having a light yellow or green skin, and pink or white edible flesh with tiny seeds.

19. A large, smooth-skinned melon with juicy pink or red flesh and black seeds.

20. A small, soft, round fruit, red or black when ripe, containing a stone. Its tree has beautiful flowers when in bloom.

10
NATURE'S BOUNTEOUS TREES

Nature is bounteous in her gift of trees to mankind. Choose the correct word from the choices given below and complete the following sentences.

1. The ________ between the main branch of a tree and its trunk remains constant in each species, and this principle applies to the principal vein of the tree's leaves and all its subsidiary branching veins.

   a. breadth

   b. length

   c. height

   d. angle

2. The Eternal God is a ________ tree in California that is believed to be at least 12,000 years old.

   a. pine

   b. redwood

   c. teak

   d. spruce

3. It is estimated that millions of trees in the world are accidentally planted by ________ who bury nuts and then forget where they hid them!

   a. squirrels

   b. natives

   c. mice

   d. birds

4. An orange tree may bear oranges for more than __________ years.

   a. 10

   b. 50

   c. 100

   d. 1,000

5. The __________ of the redwood tree is fireproof.

   a. leaf

   b. branch

   c. bark

   d. root

6. In a year, an average tree gives off enough oxygen sufficient for __________ people to breathe for a whole year.

   a. two

   b. four

   c. nine

   d. twenty

7. The bark of the __________ tree is used to prepare quinine.

   a. cinchona

   b. teak

   c. pine

   d. neem

8. The Japanese flowering cherries are __________ trees.
   a. shady
   b. wind breaking
   c. ornamental
   d. wild

9. __________ are seldom troubled by pests or diseases, and require only small amounts of feeding.
   a. magnolias
   b. ficus
   c. eucalyptus
   d. conifers

10. The fronds of the _________ palm are a greenish grey, and have a drooping appearance.
    a. jelly
    b. bungalow
    c. windmill
    d. coconut

11. The __________ gum tree is quite spectacular when in bloom with flowers of cream, or various shades of orange, pink or red during the summer.
    a. coral
    b. mallee
    c. fuchsia
    d. flowering

12. Golden wattle, silver wattle and zigzag wattle all belong to the _________ group of trees.
    a. eucalyptus
    b. teak
    c. acacia
    d. ash

13. The foliage of _________ varies greatly in form and colour, from greens to blues and golden shades, changing colour with the seasons and climatic conditions.
    a. oak
    b. conifer
    c. ash
    d. larch

14. The _________ tree is commonly found in forests, with silver grey bark and hard close-grained wood.
    a. oak
    b. conifer
    c. ash
    d. larch

15. The _________is a tall deciduous tree of the pine family with small cones and needle-like leaves.
    a. oak
    b. conifer
    c. ash
    d. larch

16. The seeds of the ripe fruit of the __________ tree is used as a creaming agent for rubber latex.
   a. tamarind
   b. neem
   c. cinchona
   d. peepal

17. The __________ is also known as the flame of the forest.
   a. jacaranda
   b. sycamore
   c. birch
   d. gulmohar

18. The __________ tree has smooth bark, shiny leaves, and small triangular nuts.
   a. jacaranda
   b. beech
   c. poplar
   d. chestnut

19. The __________ tree has smooth reddish-brown nuts enclosed in prickly cases, and its nuts are roasted and eaten.
   a. birch
   b. beech
   c. poplar
   d. chestnut

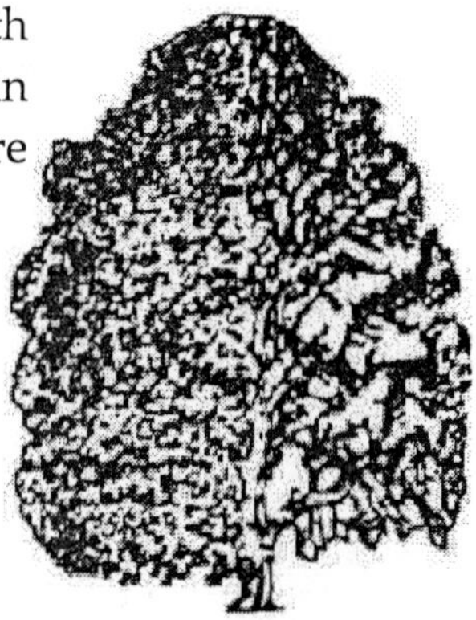

20. The wood of the __________ tree is valuable for its hard wood and the tree is a large tree of the maple family.

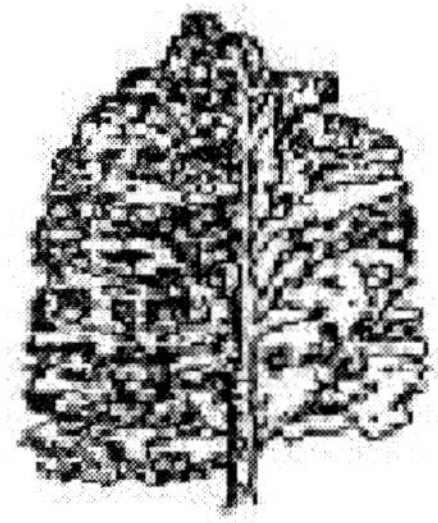

a. birch
b. sycamore
c. willow
d. oak

21. The wood of __________ tree is used especially for making cricket bats.

a. birch
b. sycamore
c. willow
d. hazel

22. The __________ tree bears cones and has needle shaped leaves, growing in clusters, which are used in the manufacture of disinfectants, soaps, perfumes, etc.

a. pine
b. spruce
c. beech
d. birch

11
WOODY FORESTS

Choose the correct answers from the choices given below to each statement.

1. The leaves of the __________ tree produces sugar.
   a. gum
   b. maple
   c. coconut
   d. redwood

2. The name given to a young tree is __________.
   a. shoot
   b. shrub
   c. lichen
   d. sapling

3. The age of a tree is estimated by counting the tree __________ on a cut stump.
   a. rings
   b. wedges
   c. barks
   d. grains

4. There are __________ types of forest fires.
   a. two
   b. three
   c. six
   d. seven

5. One-third of all the world's rainforest is in _________.
   a. India
   b. Malaysia
   c. Brazil
   d. Ghana

6. The tropical _________ is the most fertile reservoir of wildlife.
   a. rainforest
   b. zone
   c. country
   d. region

7. The study of trees as individuals in relation to their environment is known as forest _________.
   a. ecology
   b. environment
   c. biotechnology
   d. autecology

8. Eucalyptus was brought to Europe from _________.
   a. Brazil
   b. Australia
   c. South Africa
   d. Indonesia

9. The __________ is popular as Green Gold but is yet an ecological disaster.
   a. peepal
   b. neem
   c. eucalyptus
   d. pine

10. Richard St. Barbe Baker is often referred to as the Man of the __________.
    a. forests
    b. trees
    c. plants
    d. jungle

11. Among the Indian trees the most medically beneficial tree is the __________.
    a. peepal
    b. tamarind
    c. papaya
    d. neem

12. __________ forests of Asia are inhabited by snow leopards.
    a. Rain
    b. Desert
    c. Mountain
    d. Low-lying

13. Forest regions with a dense growth of trees are called __________.
    a. steppes
    b. prairies
    c. parks
    d. savannas

14. The __________ forest existed about 200 million years ago.
    a. Redwood
    b. Deciduous
    c. Jurassic
    d. Xerophyte

15. The most petrified forests lies in __________ in India and in Arizona in the United States.
    a. Bandipur
    b. Andamans
    c. Gujarat
    d. The Himalayas

16. Some of the sequoia trees of the north-western United States are more than __________ thousand years old.
    a. one
    b. two
    c. three
    d. four

17. __________ arabic is produced by several varieties of acacia trees, which grow in Africa, India and Australia.

a. Gum

b. Coffee

c. Tea

d. Paprika

18. Most of the trees of the __________ forests are evergreens like pine, spruce, fir, hemlock, etc.

a. tropical rain

b. temperate

c. coniferous

d. equatorial

19. The trees of the __________ forests shed their leaves in the cold and dry season.

a. tropical

b. temperate

c. coniferous

d. equatorial

20. The plants and trees are found in abundance in the forests, though the __________ is less.

a. grass

b. fauna

c. moisture

d. insects

12
HERBAL FARE

Unscramble the names of the following herbs.

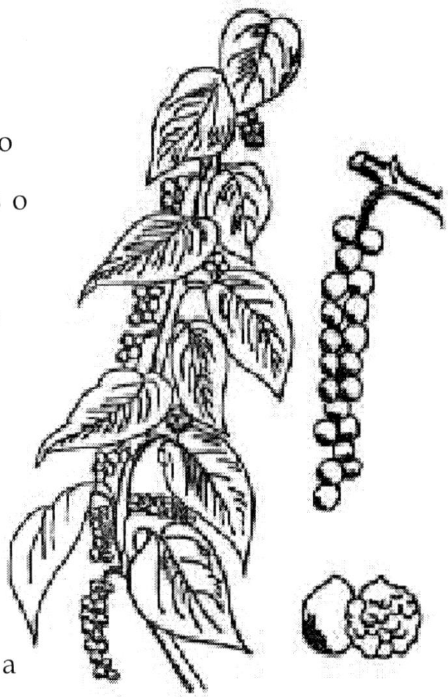

1. l i l d
2. a i s a s c
3. a a c d r m m o
4. a a a f t i e d s o
5. a i b l s
6. l u r q c i e i o
7. s a m r o g a
8. u m t g n e
9. y r m r s o e a
10. e g a s
11. s e i n d a e
12. m t s e p r i n a
13. p e e p r m t i n p
14. w r y c a a a
15. t m y e h
16. v d r e l a n e
17. g k e n f u r e e
18. r r i i c n a e a
19. l i v a l a n

20. d u l e l a c a n

21. a f o r s f n

22. f l n e n e

23. g g s e i n n

24. m m j r r a a o

25. c s u e m e i d n

26. s r l a e p y

27. c r a o t s

28. p p p e r e

29. m o m c a h i l e

30. v o l c e

13
FOUR-FOOTED ANIMALS

Most of the animals are four-footed. Some are fleet-footed, a few are wild, some fierce, etc. Can you name these animals?

1. The Gir forest in Kathiawar in India is famous for __________.
2. The __________ is the biggest and the most powerful member of the cat family.
3. In 1951, a nine-month-old __________ tiger was caught by the Maharaja of Rewa.

4. The __________ leopard lives in snow areas.

5. The __________ is the fastest-four-footed animal in the world.

6. The __________ cat is a sandy-coloured animal, slightly bigger than the domestic cat.
7. The Indian __________, slightly bigger than a jungle cat, has a long, erect tuft of hair on its ears.
8. The __________, belonging to the cat family, lives mostly in the deserts, preying on birds.
9. The __________ has been known to Indians from very ancient times because it produces a pleasant aromatic substance which is in much demand the world over for use in perfumes.
10. The __________, on occasions, keeps a heap of old bones on the ground, and dances around it, giving out a kind of hysterical laughter.
11. The Indian __________ is like a dog in appearance, very much like an Alsatian.
12. The __________ are known for their cunning and intelligence, and many stories have been written about them.
13. __________ normally hunt in pairs, living on reptiles, small animals and little birds.
14. Frequently found with snake-charmers, the __________ kills a cobra with perfect confidence.
15. The __________ has a close coat of waterproof fur, a thick and muscular tail, paddle-like feet, and whiskers of standing bristles.

16. The __________ bear has a white v-shaped mark on its chest, and is hard of hearing.
17. The ring-tailed, bright chestnut-coloured __________ in India looks like a teddy bear.
18. The __________ is the largest land animal and the oldest of all mammals.
19. The __________ has a peculiar habit of dropping its dung at the same place.
20. The __________ is an animal commonly found in Tibet and North-eastern Kashmir.
21. The __________, a heavily-built animal, is dark brown in colour, and has white markings on the lower parts of the legs.
22. The __________, a wild sheep found in Ladakh, is grey in colour which changes to a darker shade in winter.
23. The African __________ can go without water like the camel for long periods.
24. The black __________, found only in India, is a handsome animal with a shining colour, and beautiful, spiral horns.
25. In central and south India, the __________ shed their antlers between the end of March and the middle of April after which they start growing again.
26. The __________ deer is famous for its sweet-smelling substance formed inside a gland under the skin of the abdomen.
27. The common langur in India is also known as __________ monkey.

28. A __________'s stripes are as individual as human fingerprints.

29. The __________ of the rhinoceros is not a bone, it is hair.

30. The elephant has 40,000 muscles in its trunk, but not a single __________.

14
MONKEY BUSINESS

Choose the correct answer from the choices given.

1. Which is the world's smallest known monkey?
   a. The Emperor Tamarin
   b. The Japanese Macaques
   c. The Pygmy Marmoset

2. Which is the largest living member of the monkey family?
   a. The Mandrell
   b. The Red Howler
   c. The Agile Mangabey

3. What does the word Orang-utan mean?
   a. Orange monkey
   b. Man of the woods
   c. Hairy monkey

4. What does the word Langur mean?
    a. Banana-eater
    b. Red-bottomed
    c. Long-tailed
5. Which monkey of Africa communicates with its fellow monkeys by blinking its white eyelids, in a form of code?
    a. The Red Howler
    b. The Red-capped Mangabey
    c. The Agile Mangabey
6. Despite its large size and fierce looks, which member of the monkey family is a peaceable animal?
    a. Gorilla
    b. Lemur
    c. Langur

7. In which year was the Golden Bamboo Lemur discovered and identified?
    a. 1980
    b. 1984
    c. 1986
8. Name the most primitive primate in the world.
    a. Red Ukari
    b. Red Colobus
    c. Aye-aye

9. Which primate is famous for its chest-beating display?
   a. Gorilla
   b. Gibbon
   c. Colobus

10. How many races of the gorilla are found in the world?
    a. Three
    b. Seven
    c. Ten

11. What is the food habit of the gorilla?
    a. Herbivorous
    b. Carnivorous
    c. Omnivorous

12. Which monkey species builds a new nest every evening to sleep during the night?
    a. Gorilla
    b. Langur
    c. Colobus

13. Which is the most northerly living macaque on earth?
    a. Japanese Macaque
    b. Pigtailed Macaque
    c. Stump-tailed Macaque

14. Where is the proboscis monkey, called the elephant of the monkey world, found?
    a. Bermuda
    b. Borneo
    c. Brazil

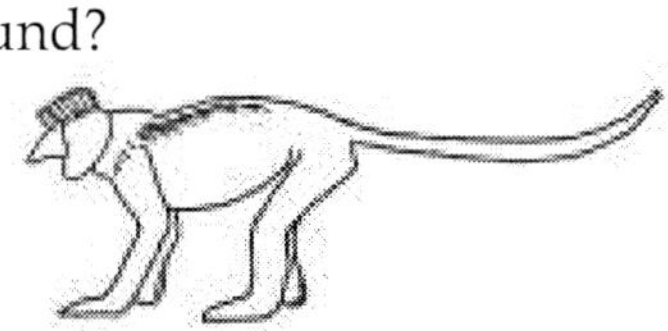

15. Which is the world's rarest monkey?
    a. Chimpanzee
    b. Lemur
    c. Gorilla

16. Which is the man-like ape found in Borneo and Sumatra?
    a. Orang-utan
    b. Langur
    c. Lemur

17. Which ape can make its own tool?
    a. Lemur
    b. Gorilla
    c. Chimpanzee

18. Which is the largest of apes?
    a. Chimpanzee
    b. Orang-utan
    c. Mountain Gorilla

19. About which of the animals do naturalists know the least?
    a. Gorillas
    b. Tapirs
    c. Baboons

20. Among the higher mammals, which is the only creature which is completely airborne?
    a. Gorilla

b. The Flying Lemus

c. Pigtailed Macaque

21. What do orang-utans use as umbrellas during a downpour?

a. Coconut shell

b. Their hands

c. Large leaves

22. Which animal has its fingerprints close to those of human beings?

a. Baboon

b. Orang-utan

c. Lemur

23. Where in India is Hoolock's Gibbon found?

a. The Western Ghats

b. The mountain forests of Assam

c. The Himalayas

24. Which animals was considered the royal and sacred creature of Thailand?

a. Siamang Gibbon

b. Slender Loris

c. Marbled Cat

25. Which primate is only found in the Rann of Kutch?

a. Hanuman Langur

b. Slender Loris

c. Lion-tailed Macaque

15
DOG MUDDLE

Given below are the names of the various breeds of dogs, but they are in a jumble. Can you unscramble the letters?

1. e g h d y r n o u

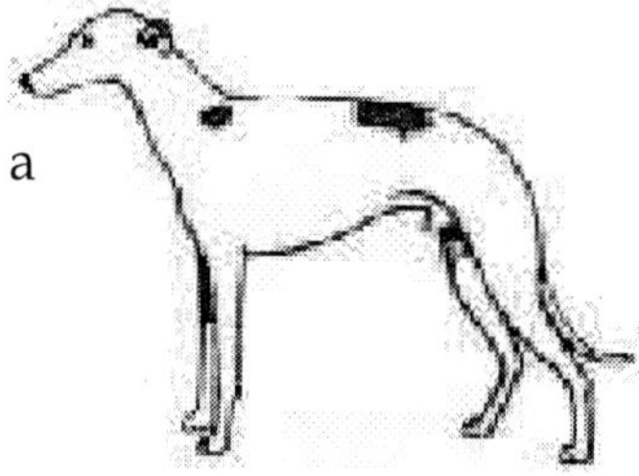

2. k c o r e c p s l i e n a
3. l o i l c e
4. a a a d l m n t i
5. e e e i k p s n

6. a a a i l n t s
7. d e o l p o
8. a a b d l r r o
9. d b g l l u o

10. a d d h h u s n c
11. d e r t e r t e s
12. t o c s h c r r e i t e r
13. e m n g r a s p e r h d h e
14. x o r e b

15. h i r i s t e t e r s

16
THE DOG FAMILY

State whether the following statements are 'True' or 'False'.

1. An Alsatian's sense of smell is a million times better than a man's.
2. Dogs sweat through their eyes.
3. A dog can hear high-frequency sounds which a human ear cannot.
4. The bat-eared fox is the only member of the dog family that thrives on insects.
5. A Prairie Dog is a wild dog.
6. The dachshund is classified under the hound species of dog.
7. The Lakeland Terrier is the largest terrier breed.
8. The Cockapu is a mixture of Cocker spaniel and Poodle.
9. The Rampur Hound comes from India.
10. French poodles originated in France.

17
FELINE GRACE

Fill in the blanks with suitable words to complete these statements about the cat family.

1. The desert __________ catches birds by leaping into the air.

2. The soles of a __________'s paws will perspire if it hears a dog barking.
3. The __________ cat has no tail.
4. The only cat that cannot retract its claws is the __________.

5. __________ are black leopards.
6. The __________ is the largest bread of domesticated cat.
7. The Asiatic __________ is the largest member of the cat family.

8. The word __________ is Latin for catlike.
9. The first white __________ to leave India for USA was purchased by Radio Corporation of America from the Maharaja of Rewa in 1960.

10. The smallest wild cat in the world is the __________ cat.
11. The __________ is known variously as puma, panther or mountain lion.

12. __________ census is used for estimating the tiger population in the wild.
13. The __________ cat has a pelt colour pattern like a panther.

14. The only country where both the lion and the tiger are found in the wild is __________.

15. The only species of cat which is a pack hunter and lives in a close-knit group is a _________.

16. As per the census in 1990, _________ is the total number of surviving Asiatic lions in the wild.

17. _________ is the place of the origin of the tiger.

18. The _________ is the largest cat of North and South America.

19. The earliest known document in India in which the white tiger is mentioned is the _________.

20. The _________ of the cat family, found in the region from Mexico and southern Brazil, has monkey-like climbing skills, and is endangered because of being hunted for its coat and loss of habitat by deforestation.

18
YOUNG ONES

Match the young ones with their parents.

A	B
1. cow	1. poult
2. rabbit	2. lamb
3. turkey	3. gosling
4. seal	4. chicken
5. swan	5. kindle
6. cat	6. kid

7. goose
8. duck

9. dog
10. horse
11. kangaroo

12. sheep

13. stallion
14. hen

15. goat
16. lion
17. partridge
18. rooster
19. fish
20. hare

21. frog

22. pigeon
23. eel
24. deer

25. pig
26. butterfly

27. hawk
28. salmon

7. calf
8. whelp
9. colt
10. cygnet
11. cheeper
12. kitten
13. duckling
14. puppy
15. cockerel
16. piglet
17. swab
18. cub
19. fawn
20. polliwog
21. foal
22. leveret
23. fingerling
24. joey
25. elver
26. bowet
27. fry
28. filly

29. trout
30. mare

29. parr
30. moth

19
HOME SWEET HOME

Home is where one is comfortable. Fill in the blanks with the names or shelters of the animals in the following sentences.

1. A pig's enclosure is called a ________.
2. A squirrel's home is called a ________.
3. The nest of a rabbit or hare is called a ________.
4. The crows, kites, doves, vultures, storks and cormorants make their nests in the ________ of the tree-trunks.
5. Quails and jungle fowls prepare scraps on the ________, lined with grass, as nests.
6. Bee-eaters, kingfishers and the hoopoe make a ________ nest in the earth banks.
7. Swallows live in ________ nests.
8. The ________ bird lives in a nest made of leaves stitched together.
9. A dog finds shelter in a ________.
10. A horse lives in a ________.
11. The cow is sheltered in a ________.

12. The house or box in which pigeons or doves are kept is called a _________.
13. The dwelling place of an animal underground is a _________.
14. The home of a lion is the _________.
15. The nesting place of a wild home is a _________.

20
MAMMALIAN ANIMALS

Spot the odd one out.

1. a. Pig
   b. Goat
   c. Whale
   d. Bandicoot

2. a. Lemur
   b. Bat
   c. Squirrel
   d. Hare

3. a. Dachshund
   b. Beagle
   c. Poodle
   d. Bloodhound

4. a. Bison
   b. Gaur
   c. Yak
   d. Gayal

5. a. Dzeggetai
   b. Kiang
   c. Khur
   d. Gaur

6. a. Desi
   b. Zebu
   c. Brahmany
   d. Nilgai

7. a. Tapir
   b. Horse
   c. Rhinoceros
   d. Armadillo

8. a. Dingo
   b. Puma
   c. Cougar
   d. Ocelot

9. a. Sambar
   b. Stag
   c. Antelope
   d. Dhole

10. a. Panther
    b. Lion-tailed Macaque
    c. Hyena
    d. Lynx

11. a. Red fox
    b. Dhole
    c. Hanuman Langur
    d. Tiger

12. a. Tahr
    b. Ibex
    c. Goral
    d. Serow

13. a. Musk Deer
    b. Barking Deer
    c. Swamp Deer
    d. Hog Deer

14. a. Black Buck
    b. Chausingha
    c. Chital
    d. Nilgai

15. a. Lynx
    b. Wolf
    c. Llama
    d. Bear

21
FEATHERED FRIENDS

Answer the following questions.

1. Which bird can sing 130 different notes in seven seconds?

2. Which bird barks like a dog?
3. Which bird flies from the Arctic round the world to the Antarctic and back again every year?
4. Which bird is faithful to its mate all its life?
5. Which bird has special combs on its toes for scratching off slime from fish?
6. Which sacred bird was believed by the ancient Egyptians to be the bird that hatched the 'world egg'?
7. Which bird of the Antarctic can reach a depth of 870 feet and remain submerged for as long as 18 minutes?
8. Which flocks of migrating birds sometimes hold a dance before flying?
9. Which bird has a night vision five times greater than a human being?
10. Which bird can swallow a hen's egg whole without breaking the shell?
11. Which bird can beat its wings 90 times a second?
12. Which bird catches fish by spearing them with its bill?
13. Which bird's beak is so sensitive that it can detect worms deep in the ground?
14. Which bird's chicks grow about one and a half metres in their first year?

15. Which bird has the largest cerebral hemispheres, relative to body size, of any avian family?

16. Which bird can eat only when its head is upside down?

17. Which bird's bones weigh less than its feathers?

18. Which bird of the snipe family has an upward-curving bill?

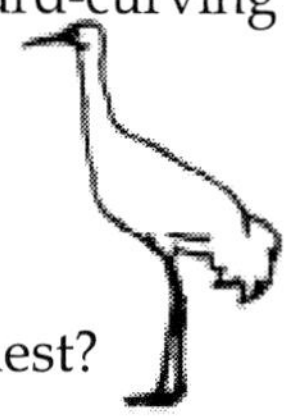

19. Which is the world's fastest flying bird?

20. Which bird displays 'bowing and beak-clattering' while changing duties at the nest?

21. Which is the bird with the longest wing span?

22. Which bird has its legs encased within the body down to the ankle joint?

23. Which bird has a tubed nose?

24. Which bird in the southern hemisphere shows remarkable resemblance to the little auk of the Arctic waters?

25. Which bird is often called the 'white-headed stork', inhabiting the papyrus marshes of the upper Nile?

26. Which group of birds lack the strengthening of the rib cage found in most of the other birds?

27. Which bird was the symbol of Roman power?

28. Which bird's nostrils open at the tip of the bill?

29. Which African bird is popularly known as a 'snake-killer'?

30. Which European bird produces 'pee-wee' calls?

22
MUDDLED BIRDS

The birds are in a muddle with their letters all mixed up. Unscramble them to find the names of the birds.

1. o d p e o w e k c r
2. a g l p i n w
3. s y a k k l r
4. s a w w o l l
5. p d r a t g i d e
6. a c c i t r n t e r
7. s e e y t a c r r d r i b
8. d o a r r r n n e u
9. k k o o a a r r u b
10. v t u u e r l
11. c l d n i a a r
12. o o i e l r
13. n g t n a e i h i g l
14. m c a a w
15. w r r l e a b
16. g l f d c i o n h
17. r n b i o
18. a e t v c o

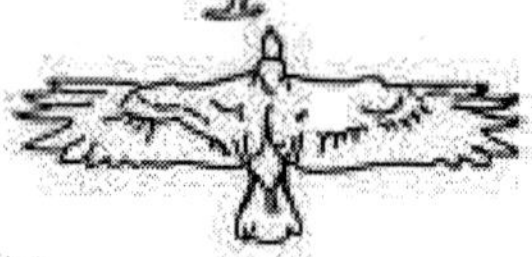

19. h l b o i l r n

20. c e h a c e k i s d

21. j a a a c n

22. m l a o n

23. h y o b b

24. s l l e b h i o

25. e e l a g

26. v o d e

27. p n i g u e n

28. o h s c t i r

29. h g u n m i m r d i b

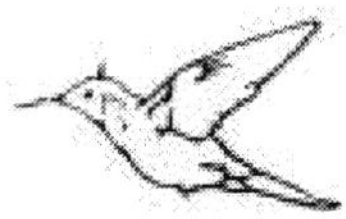

30. f n o c l a

23
BUTTERFLIES AND MOTHS

State whether the following statements are 'True' or 'False'.

1. A butterfly can look at you through 12,000 eyes.
2. The Silk Moth is not found in the wild.
3. The Alexandra Birdwing Butterfly is the largest butterly in the world.
4. The Purple Emperor is the rarest butterfly in the world.

5. The Elephant Hawk Moth is the largest moth in existence found in South-east Asia.
6. The chemical pheromone is emitted by the female moth to attract the male moths during the mating season.
7. Poison Ivy is the most preferred food, a very poisonous plant, of the Mammoth Butterfly.
8. The largest known lipidopteran is the Hawkmoth.
9. The Privet Hawkmoth has enough poison in its body to kill a medium-sized bird.
10. The Death's Head Hawkmoth sometimes sneaks into a beehive unnoticed, by mimicking the piping sound of the queen bee.
11. The Dwarf Blue is the world's smallest butterfly.
12. Red Admirals and Dingy Skippers are river crabs.
13. The Lime Hawk, Small Elephant Hawk, Garden Tiger and Green Carpets are small butterflies.
14. There are more than a hundred thousand species of moths.
15. The butterfly gets its nectar from the base of the petals.

24
INSECT LIFE

Pick the right option.

1. Fireflies are bright enough to shine through the stomach of a __________.

a. frog

b. tiger

c. lynx

d. mouse

2. The Potter __________ makes a vase-like nest of clay, then hangs the egg inside on a thread, and the vase is stocked with a caterpillar on which the larva will feed.

   a. Wasp

   b. Butterfly

   c. Bee

   d. Moth

3. A __________ insect can survive in a frozen state in the Arctic for months but dies if exposed to the warmth of a human hand.

   a. small

   b. wingless

   c. hairy

   d. large

4. __________ outnumber any other living creatures on earth.

   a. Ants

   b. Flies

   c. Mosquitoes

   d. Beetles

5. __________ are commonly called 'black beetles', but they are not black, and it is not a beetle.

   a. Dragonflies

   b. Snails

   c. Cockroaches

   d. Worms

6. The female __________ can hear her mate calling a mile away.

   a. cricket

   b. cicada

   c. wasp

   d. bee

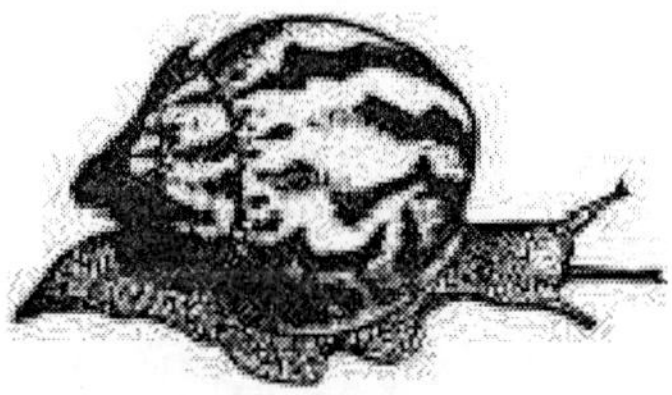

7. A __________ can crawl over a razor blade without cutting itself.

   a. cockroach

   b. worm

   c. snail

   d. ant

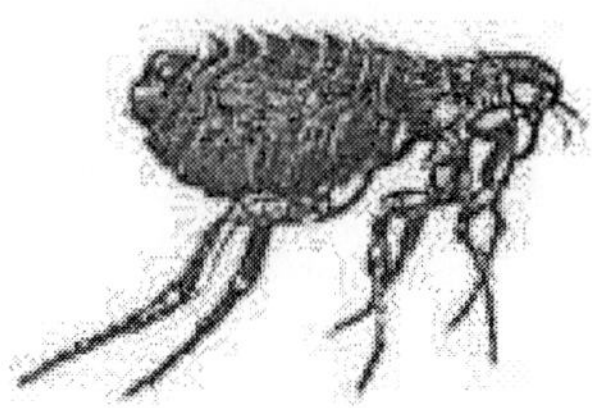

8. A __________ can jump over 200 times its own length.

   a. flea

   b. fly

   c. wasp

   d. butterfly

9. The __________ can see a flying gnat at distance of 18 feet.

a. wasp

b. bee

c. butterfly

d. dragonfly

10. The __________ butterfly makes a sound by beating the ground with one hind leg.

a. Alexandra Birdwing

b. Swallowtail

c. Large Blue

d. Birdwint

11. The largest beetle in the world is the _________ beetle.

a. Dung

b. Stag

c. Dak Bush

d. Goliath

12. The Californian petroleum __________ has its larvae living in pools of crude oil.

a. beetle

b. worm

c. fly

d. snail

13. The __________ beetle instinctively rolls balls of dung to use either for food or for laying eggs.

a. Goliath beetle

b. Stag beetle

c. Dak Bush

d. Tumblebug

14. The world's largest terrestrial snail that is over 15 cm in length is the __________.

    a. Giant African Snail

    b. Cannibal Snail

    c. Roman Snail

    d. Hylothid

15. Most ____ bees die after they sting people, as our skin is elastic and unsuitable for their stingers, and in the process their venom glands get impaired.

    a. worker

    b. queen

    c. bumble

    d. honey

16. A flea has __________ wings.

    a. two

    b. four

    c. six

    d. none

17. The __________ beetle has mandibles that enlarge into hard antlers by which they fight each other.

    a. Ladybird

    b. Stag

    c. Black

    d. Water

18. The __________ produces its song by scraping over part of the leg, called the file, against the front wing.

a. bee

b. bettle

c. cricket

d. fly

19. __________ locomote by jumping.

a. Fleas

b. Mosquitoes

c. Flies

d. Crickets

20. The principal food of the mosquitoes is __________.

a. human blood

b. plant nectar

c. garbage

d. ants

21. The __________ has two compound and three simple eyes.

a. flea

b. beetle

c. cockroach

d. mosquito

22. Formica __________ keep aphids, beetles and lice as herds, milk them, move them around, build shelters for them and supervise their grazing.

a. Ants

b. Bees

c. Beetles

d. Mosquitoes

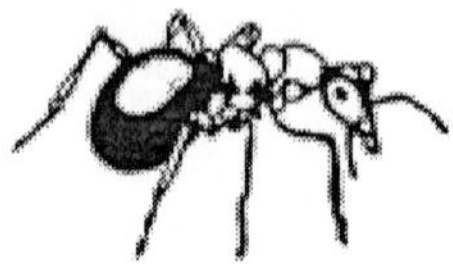

23. Overpopulation causes ________ to migrate to new lands.
    a. flies
    b. mosquitoes
    c. fleas
    d. locusts

24. The female mosquito attracts the male by its ________.
    a. wings
    b. sound
    c. sight
    d. smell

25. The ________ fly is commonly found in slaughter houses.
    a. greenbottle
    b. house
    c. stable
    d. common

26. The preferred diet of the ________ is starch and sugar.
    a. bee
    b. mosquito
    c. fly
    d. silverfish

27. Relapsing fever and typhus are spread by _________.
   a. mosquito
   b. fly
   c. headlice
   d. flea

28. The Assassin _________ prey on other insects by imitating them right down to the smallest detail.
   a. bugs
   b. lice
   c. wasps
   d. bees

29. The _________ are important agents in the biological control of mosquitoes and flies.
   a. waterbeetles
   b. bees
   c. dragonflies
   d. wasps

30. The _________ colony has a king, a queen, soldiers and workers.
   a. ant
   b. termite
   c. bee
   d. beetle

25
CREEPY CRAWLIES

Complete the statements about reptiles with the right words.

1. Turtles have no _________.
2. The longest snake is the reticulated _________ of South-east Asia, which regularly exceeds 20 feet in length.
3. A tortoise which died in 1966 was _________ years old, presented to the king of Tonga in 1773 by Captain Cook.
4. A _________'s tongue is often twice as long as its body.

5. _________ have a semi-transparent third eyelid which slides over the eyes when they are submerged.
6. The stump-tailed _________ of Australia has a tail that looks like its head.

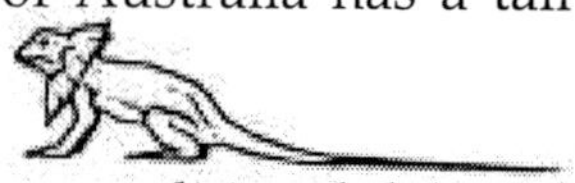

7. The Green _________ provides a traditional delicacy at wedding feasts in Papua New Guinea.
8. The _________ snake releases bad-smelling chemicals of stink glands, and in extreme cases shams dead, as methods of self-defence.
9. The Aldabra Islands in the Indian Oceans, off the coast of East Africa, are famous for some 150,000 giant _________.
10. The largest snake is the _________.

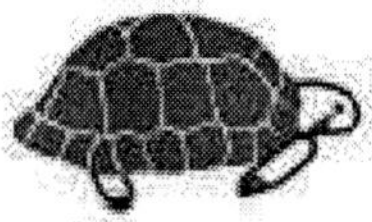

11. The __________ kills its prey by curling round it, suffocating and swallowing whole.

12. The __________ snakes obtain food by striking, biting and venom injection.

13. The __________ avoids being overheated in the deserts by sheltering in the shade, raising the belly off the ground, and having the ability to survive higher body temperature.

14. The marine __________, found in the Galapagos Islands, thrives in marine rocky coasts.

15. Destruction of marshy lakes, and hunting for skin are the main threats to the survival of the American __________.

16. The largest crocodile is the __________ Crocodile.

17. The long-snouted crocodile or ____________ is distinguished from the marsh and estuarine crocodile by its long snout, and is a fish-eater.

18. The nest-site of the sea __________ is beaches with light sand.

19. The food of the giant tortoise is __________.

20. The largest turtle in the world is the __________.

26
THE AMPHIBIANS

The amphibians live in water and on land. State whether the following statements about them are true or false.

1. The tree toad of Martinique climbs tree with its young clinging to its back.
2. The horned toad looks ferocious, but has a mild disposition, and makes a good pet.
3. The eggs of the female Goeldi's frog of South America are held on her back in folds of skin.
4. The male midwife toad carries the eggs laid by its mate like a bunch of grapes attached to its back.
5. The Spring Peeper is the smallest of all frogs measuring only one inch.
6. The Salamander Oxolotyl is an amphibian called Peter Pan because it is very small.
7. Salamanders, newts and sirens have tails.
8. Toads are used in Unani medicine.
9. The most venomous amphibian in the world is the Fire-bellied Toad.
10. The largest amphibian in the world is the Chinese Giant Salamander.

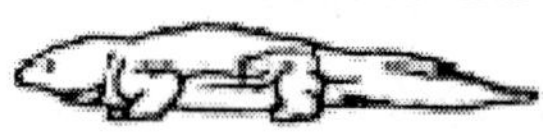

11. The Alpine Salamander is found only in Ezell's Cave near San Marcos in Texas that, unlike other members of the group, retains gills throughout its life for breathing.
12. Tree frogs move by jumping.
13. A frog breathes under water through its skin.
14. A tadpole has a neck and a tail.
15. A female frog has highly developed vocal cords.

27
MOLLUSCS

Molluscs are a group of animals with soft bodies that are covered with hard shells composed of calcium carbonate. Given below are some of the molluscs that are all in a jumble. Can you unscramble them?

1. e r y t o s
2. m l a c
3. o s u p o t c
4. s u m e s l
5. i l s n a
6. s i d q u
7. f c t l u s e h i t
8. s g u l

28
FISHY TALES

The clues indicate facts about fishes.

1. This fish has a glowing rod over its mouth which attracts smaller fish that are snapped up by the sharp teeth.
2. This fish of Thailand builds its nest underwater, bringing air from the surface and saliva to create a nest of bubbles.

3. It can hit an insect up to 122 cm away with drops of water squirted from its mouth.
4. Though only 23 cm long, this fish can kill crocodiles.
5. This fish, found in the Mississippi river, catches food merely by swimming along it with its mouth open.
6. It weighs 5,000 times as much as its brain.
7. This fish of the American Pacific is so oily that the Indians tie them to sticks to make torches.
8. This fish carries her tiny husband attached to her undersides.
9. This fish, found in the South American seas, is a very vicious and bloodthirsty fish.
10. This fish hangs a bait for its prey.
11. It is used to catch turtles.
12. This eel, found in South American rivers, can discharge almost 400-500 volts from its tail, and can kill a person on contact.
13. Called the Portuguese man-of-war, this fish, like a floating colony of polyps, has stinging tentacles that are very poisonous.
14. This fish has three separate hearts.
15. This is the name given to about 20 species of salt water carnivorous fishes with a big jaw and teeth.
16. These fishes, belying their names, do not fly, but slide propelled by their tails and leap into the air, using the front fins as wings.

17. This fish breathes air directly with its swim bladder that functions like a lung.
18. This is the only fish that makes a nest.
19. These fishes are found in tropical Africa.
20. This fish, only 8 mm long, is the shortest fish.
21. This fish can lay the most eggs.
22. This fish is very valuable as its eggs are eaten as caviar.
23. This fish can leap out of the water, squirt its prey, and knock it down.
24. This has three rows of teeth.
25. This fish has the longest snout.
26. This is the strangest fish in the seabed, living on the leftovers that fall from above.
27. This fish has the longest lifespan of 50 to 80 years.
28. This fish resembles a shark but has a body shaped like a guitar, often found in the Mumbai seacoast.
29. This male fish entangles the egg mass on a hook like process on its head until they are hatched ___ found in New Guinea.
30. This fish carries its eggs in its month.
31. This fish's skin is used as leather for covering jewel-boxes, fine books and sword handles.
32. Which fish is known as the king of fishes?

33. This fish ranks first as an animal to have the most taste buds – 27,000 taste buds.

34. This fish is apparently the only animal that never falls sick, and is immune to every known disease.

35. This fish loses its colour if kept in dim light, or placed in a body of running water, such as a stream.

36. This female fish lays about 500,000 eggs at one time.

37. This fish lays approximately 14 million eggs during its lifetime.

38. This fish has a memory span of three seconds.

39. This fish causes enormous damage to the coral reef during its feeding.

40. This fish is used as a decoy to trap dolphins.

41. This fish is popularly known as Zebrafish, Dragonfish or Devilfish.

42. This fish is multi-coloured.

43. This exotic fish poses a danger to the survival of the viviparous fish found in the Big Bend National Park of Texas.

44. This fish comprises four hearts, a nostril, no jaw or stomach, and scavenges on dead animals.

45. This fish lays eggs inside the mantle of freshwater mussels.

46. This is the largest marine flatfish.

47. This fish attaches itself to large sea creatures, and eats from the bits of fish that escape from their mouths.

48. This is the most widely eaten fish in India.

49. This fish in India has functionless gills, walks on the sand with its pectoral fine, and rests on the branches of mangrove plants.

50. This fish cleans the mouths of other fish of parasites and infected tissue.

29
MARINE LIFE

State whether the following statements about marine life are true or false.

1. Hundreds of fossil jellyfish found in Australia prove that the area was covered by the sea 600 million years ago.
2. A single oyster lays 500 million eggs a year, yet only one of them will normally reach maturity.
3. The jellyfish has no skeleton.
4. The aquatic animal with the most developed intelligence is the whale.
5. Walrus, whales and dolphins are aquatic animals.
6. The sperm whale has the biggest whale.

7. The porpoise is the smallest of the whale family.
8. The tusks of the walrus are used for making ornaments.
9. Dolphins navigate and hunt by making distinctive sounds.

10. Seals can sleep under water, but they have to wake up every few minutes to surface and breathe.

11. A squid seizes its prey with its suckers, and then paralyses it with a deadly nerve poison.

12. The gestation period of a dolphin is 360 days.

13. Seasponges are plants in the sea.

14. A dogfish is a kind of fish that lives in shallow waters.

15. The Narwhal, known as the unicorn of the seas, has a horn growing out of its forehead.

16. A sand dollar is a sea urchin that has short spines, and a very flattened skeleton, making it look like a biscuit or a large coin.

16. There are about 200 species of starfishes in the world.

17. It takes a lobster approximately one year to grow to be one pound.

18. The wedded seal, which is the deepest diver of all seals, can stay submerged for an hour.

19. The only sea mammal that lacks thick blubber is the killer whale.

20. The hermit crab does not have its own shell but moves about in the empty shells of whales that it occupies temporarily.

21. Fossilised sea shells found on Mount Everest show that the Himalayas were once part of the sea floor.

22. Wading birds used their long beaks for finding worms in the sand.

23. Life on earth started in the sea over 3,500 million years ago.

24. Sting rays have poisonous spines on the end of their long, whip-like tails.

25. The crown of thorns starfish can eat 300-400 sq cms of coral in a day.

30
GROUPS OF ANIMALS

Most animals live in groups. Given below is a list of some of the most interesting and unusual groups, but it is incomplete. So, get ready and fill up the blank spaces.

1. A __________ of ants
2. A __________ of bees
3. An __________ of caterpillars
4. A __________ of locusts
5. A __________ of bass
6. A __________ of fish
7. A __________ of jellyfish
8. A __________ of trout
9. A __________ of whales
10. A __________ of chickens
11. A __________ of crows

12. A __________ of doves

13. A __________ of geese

14. A __________ of hens

15. A __________ of lapwings

16. An __________ of larks

17. A __________ of nightingales

18. A __________ of owls

19. A __________ of partridges

20. An __________ of peacocks

21. An __________ of ravens

22. A __________ of rooks

23. A __________ of sparrows

24. A __________ of starlings

25. A __________ of storks

26. A __________ of swallows

27. A __________ of turkeys

28. A __________ of woodpeckers

29. A __________ of snipe

30. A __________ of apes

31. A __________ of badgers

32. A __________ of bears

33. A __________ of cats

34. A _______ of cattle
35. A _______ of foxes
36. A _______ of hares
37. A _______ of hawks
38. A _______ of herons
39. A _______ of horses
40. A _______ of kittens
41. A _______ of leopards
42. A _______ of lions
43. A _______ of oxen
44. A _______ of ponies
45. A _______ of puppies
46. A _______ of rabbits
47. A _______ of rhinoceros
48. A _______ of seals
49. A _______ of sheep
50. A _______ of squirrels
51. A _______ of toads
52. A _______ of turtledoves
53. A _______ of turtles
54. A _______ of wolves

31
PLACID LAKES

Given below are the names of some well-known and lesser known lakes, and the countries in which they are found. Match them.

Lakes	Countries / Continents
1. Caspian	1. Africa
2. Superior	2. USA
3. Victoria	3. China
4. Chilika Lake	4. Uganda
5. Constance	5. Asia
6. Koko Nor	6. India
7. Masurian Lakes	7. USA-Canada
8. Baikal	8. Orissa, India
9. Eyre	9. Italy
10. Nasser	10. Hungary
11. Great Salt Lake	11. Switzerland
12. Garda	12. Russia
13. Albert	13. Australia
14. Balaton	14. Poland
15. Dal	15. Egypt

32
GUSHING RIVERS

How well do you know the names of rivers of the world?

1. Which is the longest river in the world?
   a. Missouri
   b. Nile
   c. Amazon
   d. Yangtze Kiang

2. Which river is called the sorrow of China?
   a. Yangtze Kiang
   b. Yanisey
   c. Hwangho
   d. Yukon

3. On which river is Berlin situated?
   a. Spree
   b. Odor
   c. Rhine
   d. Rhone

4. Which is the longest river is Europe?
   a. Seine
   b. Rhine
   c. Danube
   d. Volga

5. From where does the Ganges originate?
   a. Yamanotri
   b. Gangotri
   c. Talacauvery
   d. Aravali mountains

6. Which Chinese city lies on the Waterloo river?
   a. Beijing
   b. Canton
   c. Shanghai
   d. Nankin

7. Which highly polluted Italian river discharges 234 tonnes of arsenic into the sea a year?
   a. Po
   b. Arno
   c. Tiber
   d. Adda

8. Which river's fertile data in south China is known as the 'Land of fish, rice and fruit"?
   a. Yangtze
   b. Pearl river
   c. Hwangho
   d. Ob

9. Which Indian city is situated on the Ganges river?
   a. Varanasi
   b. Agra

c. Lucknow
d. Delhi

10. Which river has its origin in Lake Mansarovar and drains into the Bay of Bengal? In its long winding route it is called by five different names.
    a. Ganges
    b. Yamuna
    c. Alaknanda
    d. Brahmaputra

11. Which river flows through London?
    a. Thames
    b. Severn
    c. Trent
    d. Dee

12. The Ural, Yenisey and Lena are all rivers running entirely through one country. Name the country.
    a. Poland
    b. Rumania
    c. Russia
    d. Bulgaria

13. Which is the largest river, and which carries more water than any other river in the world?
    a. Nile
    b. Yangtze Kiang
    c. Amazon
    d. Mississippi

14. Which beautiful river inspired Johann Strauss to compose the famous waltz music?

    a. Thames
    b. Danube
    c. Volga
    d. Rhine

15. New York stands at the mouth of which river?

    a. St. Lawrence
    b. Potomac
    c. Delaware
    d. Hudson

16. Which is the longest river in the British Isles?

    a. Thames
    b. Shannon
    c. Dee
    d. Trent

17. Which African river is famous for its waterfalls?

    a. Congo
    b. Nile
    c. Zambezi
    d. Niger

18. Which Spanish-named river flows through the United States and Mexico?

    a. La Plata
    b. Orinoco

c. Rio Grande
d. Magdalena

19. Which river runs through the Grand Canyon in the United States?
    a. Hudson
    b. Colorado
    c. Platte
    d. Rio Grande

20. Which is Canada's longest river?
    a. Mackenzie
    b. Yukon
    c. Athabasca
    d. Peace

21. Which river in Africa has the largest delta?
    a. Congo
    b. Zambezi
    c. Niger
    d. Nile

22. Which river is the longest in Australia that dries up in winter?
    a. Darling
    b. Georgina
    c. Mulligan
    d. Gilbert

23. Which river flows through a region in Pakistan where once stood a famous ancient civilisation by the same name?
   a. Jhelum
   b. Sutlej
   c. Indus
   d. Helmand

24. What is the name given to River Brahmaputra in Bangladesh?
   a. Padma
   b. Karatoya
   c. Barak
   d. Kanasa

25. Which river is spanned by more than thirty bridges in Paris?
   a. Seine
   b. Loire
   c. Marne
   d. Yonne

26. Which river finds frequent mention in the *Bible*?
   a. Nile
   b. Thames
   c. Jordan
   d. Euphrates

27. Which short river flows through two countries in North America and is famous for its falls?
   a. Niagara
   b. Colorado
   c. Hudson
   d. St. Lawrence

28. Which river in Ireland flows into the Irish Sea, and on whose banks a famous battle was fought?
   a. Shannon
   b. Boyne
   c. Blackwater
   d. Noire

29. Which river forms a boundary between north-east China and North Korea, and flows into the Yellow Sea?
   a. Yalu
   b. Amur
   c. Liao ho
   d. Hwangho

30. Which river is one of the world's longest river which flows from the Atlai mountains and is crossed by the Trans-Siberian railway at Nevosibirsk?
   a. Amur
   b. Yenisey
   c. Ob
   d. Lena

33
SALTY SEAS

While some seas are calm and beautiful on some days, the same seas may turn choppy and stormy. Given below are details about them. State whether they are true or false.

1. On the island of Euboea in the Aegean Sea there is a channel of water which mystifies scientists. The current actually reverses its direction 14 times every day.
2. The Dead Sea lies between Egypt and Saudi Arabia.
3. The Caribbean Sea is the largest sea in the world.
4. The Bering Sea lies between Aleutian Islands and the strait that divides Alaska and Russia.
5. The Caribbean Sea, part of the Atlantic Ocean, between West Indies and South America, is a warm sea that is entirely within the tropics.
6. The Mediterranean Sea is almost tideless.
7. The Sea of Okhotsk is enclosed by China, North Korea and South Korea.
8. The Yellow Sea is also known as the Hwangho Sea.
9. The White Sea receives the waters of the Danube, Dneister, Dneiper, Don and Bug.

11. The Red Sea is an extension of Great African Rift valley which further north enclosed the Dead Sea.
12. There is enough salt in the sea to cover the land with a layer 153 metres thick.

13. The sea is blue because it reflects the colour of the seabed.

14. When the sea was first formed it was hot, only a few degrees below boiling point, and as acidic as lemon juice!

15. Sea water contains sodium, chlorine, calcium, magnesium, and even traces of arsenic and gold.

34
DEEP OCEANS

The oceans and seas together form one big stretch of water that flows continually around the world. Fill in the blanks to complete the sentences on oceans.

1. The largest and deepest ocean is the __________ Ocean.
2. The coldest and the smallest ocean is the __________ Ocean.
3. The Red Sea in the __________ Ocean has the saltiest sea water in the world.
4. The warmest ocean is the __________ Ocean.
5. The __________ Ocean is dotted with thousands of icebergs, with up to 15,000 new ones being formed each year.
6. No mammalian life other than whales are found in the __________ Ocean.
7. The deepest point in the __________ Ocean, and on earth, is Marianas French, at 11,034 metres.

8. Many seaquakes happen in the 'Ring of Fire' around the __________ Ocean.
9. The highest mountain on earth is not Mt Everest, but Mt__________ in the Pacific Ocean.
10. On 23 January 1960, a bathyscaphe called __________ reached the bottom of the Marianas French in the Pacific Ocean.
11. The *Marie Celeste* was a large ship found on 3 December 1872 drifting in the __________ Ocean, with all of the crew completely vanished, leaving their breakfast half-eaten on the table!
12. The __________ __________ is a large area of the Atlantic Ocean that stretches between Bermuda, Puerto Rico and Florida where ships and aircraft have mysteriously gone missing without a trace.
13. Legend has it the beautiful island of__________ sank without a trace with all its inhabitants after a massive volcanic eruption.
14. The __________ __________ is a large, natural current which occurs about every five years in the Pacific Ocean, causing the sea level to fall, the water temperature to rise, torrential rain to fall, and coral reefs to die.
15. The longest ocean swim was undertaken by Walter Poenisch in the __________ Ocean in July 1978.
16. The white foam that forms on the crests of waves in seas and oceans is often called __________ __________.
17. The deepest part of the Indian Ocean is the __________ French.

18. The __________ is the instrument used for measuring the depth of an ocean.

19. Approximately __________ per cent of the earth's total water supply is contained in the oceans.

20. The band of ocean between 50 degrees South and 69 degrees South is known as the __________ __________.

21. A Gulf Stream is another word for ocean __________.

22. __________ Ocean is the third largest one in the world.

23. The cold, salty water left behind when __________ is formed in the Arctic or Antarctic Ocean sinks right to the bottom of the bed.

24. The __________ water in the ocean is found in the tropics.

25. The famous __________ __________ was discovered by Benjamin Franklin.

26. Many surface currents such as the Gulf Stream have currents flowing beneath them, and are called __________.

27. The __________ starts in the Atlantic Ocean near the equator, then pushes the warm salty water past the Caribbean Islands into the great bay made by Florida and the east coast of the United States past Cape Hatteras.

28. The __________ sounder makes it easy to find the depth of the ocean or sea.

29. The __________ __________ of the ocean is free for all the countries to navigate.

30. In the Arctic Ocean, only one-_________ of an iceberg is every visible above the sea's surface.

35
CASCADING FALLS

Choose the right word from the options given to find the answers to the following clues.

1. The highest falls in Venezuela are at over 900 metres high.
   a. Angel Falls
   b. Jog Falls
   c. Tugela Falls
2. The Jim Jim Falls in the Alligator Rivers Wildlife Sanctuary is in _________.
   a. California
   b. Australia
   c. Norway
3. The Mardalsfossen Falls belongs to _________.
   a. Guyana
   b. Norway
   c. Venezuela
4. The Tugela Falls is in _________.
   a. South Africa
   b. France
   c. Switzerland

5. The Cuquenan Falls is in _________.
    a. Switzerland
    b. Zambia
    c. Venezuela
6. The Southerland Falls is in _________.
    a. New Zealand
    b. California
    c. Venezuela
7. The Ribbon Falls is in _________.
    a. Venezuela
    b. New Zealand
    c. California
8. The Great Kamarang Falls is in _________.
    a. Guyana
    b. Zambia
    c. Zimbabwe
9. These falls contain small volumes of water.
    a. Cataracts
    b. Cascades
    c. Rapids
10. The base of a waterfall is known as a _________ pool.
    a. fault
    b. profile
    c. plunge

11. The Della Falls is in _________.
    a. California
    b. Austria
    c. British Columbia

12. A _________ is a series of waterfalls.
    a. Catacomb
    b. Catamaran
    c. Cataract

13. The Niagara Falls between the United States of America and Canada are separated by _________ Islands.
    a. Queen Charlotte
    b. Prince of Wales
    c. Goat

14. _________ is another term for long cracks in the layers of rock upon which the waters of the waterfalls gush down.
    a. Profile
    b. Rapids
    c. Faults

15. The Trummelbach Falls lies in _________.
    a. Switzerland
    b. Norway
    c. New Zealand

16. The Jog Falls is in _________ State in India.
    a. Maharashtra
    b. Karnataka
    c. Tamil Nadu

17. The Gavarnie Falls is in _________
    a. Austria
    b. France
    c. Guyana

18. The Krimmel Falls is in _________
    a. Austria
    b. France
    c. Switzerland

19. The _________ Falls can be seen from both Canada and USA.
    a. Angel
    b. Victoria
    c. Niagara

20. The King George Falls is located in _________.
    a. Guyana
    b. Zambia
    c. Zimbabwe

36
BARREN DESERTS

State whether the following facts about deserts are true or false.

1. The Sahara is as large as Europe and larger than the combined area of the next nine largest deserts in the world.
2. One-fourth of the earth's surface is covered by desert.
3. To be classified as a desert, there must be less than 300 mm of rainfall annually.
4. Approximately 70 per cent of our desert areas are sandy, while other larger areas of desert are covered in rocks and gravel.
5. The most arid continent on earth is Africa.
6. The Nile and Niger rivers both cross the Sahara Desert.
7. The euphorbia is a cactus-like plant that grows in African deserts.
8. Camels can drink water weighing a quarter of their body weight.
9. In the Sahara Desert, 200 species of plants can be found.
10. The Sahara Desert which covers 85 per cent of the nation lies in Algeria in North Africa.
11. The Nagev Desert is located in Jordan.
12. Mangolia's greatest desert is the Gobi.

13. The Mojava Desert is in Mexico.
14. The Atacama Desert in Chile is the driest place in the world.
15. The Thar Desert between India and Pakistan is barren, has no rivers, and has no level land.
16. The Kalahari Desert lies between the rivers Limpopo and Zambezi.
17. A Mexican desert dweller lives in an adobe, a mud house that provides insulation from heat.
18. A mound of loose, dry sand formed by the wind, and changing forms very often is called a dune.
19. The Sonoran Desert with enclosed basins and salt marshes is in Australia.
20. The Takla Makan Desert is in Pakistan.

37
THE PEAKS

Name the countries where these beautiful mountain peaks are found.

1. Everest
2. Godwin-Austen or K2
3. Kanchenjunga
4. Lhotse
5. Makalu
6. Dhaulagiri

7. Nanga Parbat
8. Annapurna
9. St Elias
10. Xixabangma Feng or Gosainthan
11. Nanda Devi
12. Rakaposhi
13. Kilimanjaro
14. Mount Carmel
15. Mt McKinley
16. Jungfrau
17. Ararat
18. Mt Olympus
19. Mont Blanc
20. Matterhorn

38
THE HIGHLANDS

Choose the correct option and fill in the blanks in the sentences about mountains, hills and plateaus.

1. On the __________ mountain in Switzerland, there is a hall of ice containing piano, stove and tables, carved out of solid ice.
   a. Mont Blanc
   b. Jungfrau
   c. Matterhorn

2. The chief mountain ranges dividing France and Spain are the __________.
   a. Alps
   b. Apenines
   c. Pyrenees

3. The Himalayas are __________ type of mountains.
   a. Volcanic
   b. Block
   c. Fold

4. The Vosges in __________ is a mountain of the block type.
   a. Germany
   b. France
   c. Switzerland

5. The __________ in Japan is a volcanic mountain.
   a. Fujiyama
   b. Asahidake
   c. Fujisan

6. The Catskill mountains of New York are __________ type of mountains.
   a. volcanic
   b. fold
   c. residual

7. The _________ range is the mountain range of Antarctica.
   a. Neo-Antarctican
   b. Trans-Antarctican
   c. Snowy-Antarctican

8. The Apenines mountains range is known as the 'backbone' of _________.
   a. Switzerland
   b. Italy
   c. Austria

9. The Ben Nevis mountains in _________ is volcanic, and the highest peak in the British Isles.
   a. Scottland
   b. England
   c. Wales

10. The _________ mountain range in Europe is an arc of mountains having oilfields.
    a. Pyrenees
    b. Apenine
    c. Carpathian

11. The Hekla mountain, being volcanic, erupted in 1970 in _________.
    a. Iceland
    b. Greenland
    c. Siberia

12. The __________ mountains separate Russia from Georgia in Asia.
   a. Ural
   b. Caucasus
   c. Sayan

13. The __________ is the highest peak in the Pennine Alps on the border of Italy and Switzerland.
   a. Monte Rosa
   b. Monte Cristo
   c. Monte Carlo

14. The Montserrate mountain is in __________, and there is a Benedictine monastery on it.
   a. France
   b. Spain
   c. Portugal

15. The Stromboli is an active volcanic mountain in the Stromboli Island of __________.
   a. Greece
   b. Spain
   c. Italy

16. The Parnassus mountain ridge with its highest peak Licoreia is in __________.
   a. Greece
   b. Spain
   c. Italy

17. The Deccan Plateau in India is bounded by the Narmada and _________ rivers.
   a. Krishna
   b. Godavari
   c. Cauvery

18. _________ is an inactive volcanic mountain with many glaciers, and situated in Oregon.
   a. Mt Olympus
   b. Mt McKinley
   c. Mt Hood

19. Noah's Ark is believed to have rested on _________.
   a. Mt Logan
   b. Mt Ararat
   c. Mt Hood

39
STEAMY VOLCANOES

Put together the dislocated names of these volcanoes.

1. Mt	1. ama
2. Et	2. kono
3. As	3. go
4. Bro	4. ba
5. Can	5. Hood
6. Du	6. laon

7. Eg	7. na
8. Fo	8. la
9. Gama	9. car
10. Hek	10. oni
11. Ka	11. tombo
12. Las	12. mo
13. Momo	13. aro
14. Pip	14. Helens
15. Ruby	15. lama
16. Mount St.	16. boli
17. Santa	17. Sister
18. South	18. vius
19. Strom	19. Seamount
20. Vesu	20. Maria

40
THE QUAKES

Fill in the blanks to complete the sentences about earthquakes.

1. Thirty thousand people died in an earthquake which hit the city of St __________ on the Caribbean island of Martinique in 1908, in which the only survivor was a prisoner in the city's gaol.

2. The two kinds of earthquake are volcanic and __________.
3. The earthquake is measured by using the __________ Scale and Mercalli Scale.
4. The regions which are prone to earthquake are called __________ Belts.
5. The __________ Scale is used to assess the effects of a quake at a particular place, rather than to measure the overall power.
6. The worst earthquake disaster ever recorded so far was in the Shanshi and Honan provinces of __________ on February 2, 1556 which is estimated to have killed more than 830,000 people.
7. The place of origin of an earthquake is known as its __________.
8. The __________ causes for earthquake are filling of very large dams, direct injection of fluids into the ground, underground nuclear explosion.
9. The __________ is a point at which an earthquake occurs, and is also known as hypocentre.
10. The three types of earthquakes are shallow, __________ and deep.
11. When an earthquake strikes, tremors spread around in __________ waves.
12. __________ first detected the seismic waves.
13. The quake in 1755 destroyed and flooded __________ in Europe.

14. __________ volcano in Hawaii is the largest volcano on earth in terms of volume and height above its base.

15. Most earthquakes occur at depths of less than __________ miles from the earth's surface.

16. Near the earthquake's epicentre, the sea floor rises and falls, pushing all the matter above it up and down – this motion produces a seawave that travels in all directions, commonly as a __________.

17. In an earthquake in __________ in 1906, a great fire followed the quake, in which seven hundred people died and there was heavy property damage amounting to $ 425,000,000.

18. An earthquake that took place in __________ in 1923 killed more than one hundred thousand persons and destroyed this city in Asia.

19. This quake in __________ in 1920 covered more than three hundred square miles, and killed about two hundred thousand peoples.

20. There were 1,874 separate earthquake shocks felt in 1811 and 1812 in __________, and some of the shocks were felt four hundred miles away, but this area was sparsely settled, so not much damage was done.

41
LUSTROUS METALS

State whether the following statements about metals are true or false.

1. According to the fossils of older civilisations, perhaps gold was the first metal discovered by man.
2. Silver has a property of purifying water.
3. Wrought iron is considered the best among all forms of iron.
4. Copper becomes black by the reaction of air.
5. Manganese is added to steel to harden it and to make it more resistant to wear and tear.
6. Cassiterite is the main ore of tin found in maximum quantity in Malaysia, Indonesia, Thailand and Nigeria.
7. Mercury expands on heating and contracts on cooling.
8. The percentage of lithium in the earth's crust is very small—0.0065 per cent.
9. Beryl is found in nature in the form of large ores.
10. Lead is found in large quantities in Australia and Russia.

42
HOMOGENEOUS MINERALS

Pick the odd one out.

1. graphite
   alabaster
   bauxite
   copper

2. malachite
   bauxite
   lead
   quartz

3. mica
gypsum
aalite
copper

4. asbestos
mica
galena
iron

5. dolomite
manganese
graphite
quartz

6. alabaster
gypsum
bronze
calcite

7. cinnabar
silver
bauxite
serpentine

8. platinum
fluorite
malachite
amphibola

9. graphite
bauxite
gypsum
uranium

10. cinnabar
mica
aluminium
aalite

43
AN AMALGAMATION OF METALS-MINERALS

1. Which is the most abundant metal in the earth's crust?
   a. iron
   b. lead
   c. copper
   d. aluminium

2. Which mineral is nicknamed 'fool's gold' because its yellow colour often confuses gold prospectors?
   a. pyrite
   b. galena
   c. fluorite
   d. silica

3. Plants are not able to get nitrogen from air to produce proteins when a metal is not present in very minute quantities. Name the metal.
   a. copper
   b. gallium
   c. zirconium
   d. molybdenum

4. Which mineral ore forms kidney-shaped crystals?
   a. pyrite
   b. silica
   c. haematite
   d. galena

5. Name the metal that is as strong as steel but only half its weight.
   a. tungsten
   b. titanium
   c. uranium
   d. platinum

6. Where do natural diamonds occur?
   a. aalite
   b. pyrite
   c. covellite
   d. kimberlite

7. Which is the first alloy, a mixture of two metals, to be made in the world?
   a. bronze
   b. brass
   c. stainless steel
   d. copper

8. Which mineral is used in making plaster and paper?
   a. feldspar
   b. gypsum
   c. granite
   d. halite

9. Where in the world would you find the largest deposit of gold?
   a. Ballarat, Australia
   b. Witwatersrand, South Africa
   c. Kolar, India
   d. Muruntau, Russia

10. Which numeral is often used as an abrasive?
    a. breccia
    b. shale
    c. corundum
    d. garnet

11. Where was the technique of powder metallurgy invented?
   a. India
   b. Germany
   c. Japan
   d. England

12. Which mineral gets deposited as 'furs' in boiling pots, kettles, etc., in regions where hard-water is used?
   a. fluorite
   b. pyrite
   c. granite
   d. calcite

13. Which is the metal that remains liquid at room temperature?
   a. mercury
   b. magnesium
   c. molybdenum
   d. platinum

14. Which mineral was used for making compasses in ancient days?
   a. haemalite
   b. magnelite
   c. habite
   d. pyrite

15. Which metals are used in making the bronze alloy?
    a. zinc, tin, copper
    b. zinc, tin, aluminium
    c. tin, aluminium, nickel
    d. aluminium, nickel, zinc

16. Which type of rocks is used for roofing houses?
    a. granite
    b. slate
    c. basalt
    d. feldspar

17. Which element imparts corrosion-resistance to metal?
    a. tungsten
    b. nitrogen
    c. magnesium
    d. nickel

18. Which mineral is used in jewellery?
    a. mica
    b. halite
    c. garnet
    d. breccia

19. Even the so-called pure gold contains a metal in small amount. Name it.
    a. sodium
    b. copper
    c. tin
    d. aluminium

20. Which rock is used as stones for building houses?
    a. shale
    b. granite
    c. oolite
    d. slate

21. Which is the most widely used metal?
    a. iron
    b. gold
    c. copper
    d. aluminium

22. Which natural source will be tapped for the large-scale extraction of valuable metals in the near future?
    a. polymetallic modules
    b. red sea muds
    c. coral reefs
    d. volcanic ash

23. Which metal container is least affected by acids present in foods?
    a. iron
    b. copper
    c. aluminium
    d. zinc

44
OUR ECOSYSTEM

Complete these sentences about our ecosystem. Clues are given below.

1. The forests in Amazonia are famous for _________ forests.
2. Reef destruction, pollution and over-exploitation of living resources are threatening our _________ environment.
3. Defencelessness as a result of heavy body and flightlessness was the reason for the extinction of the _________ in Mauritius.
4. The deepest lake in the world is Lake_________.
5. Spawning nurseries for fish breeding, productive ecosystems supporting various foodchains, and groundwater recharge are the most important ecological functions of the_________.
6. The Pampas _________ is the largest South American grassland mammal.
7. The most preferred habitat for the giraffe and the African elephant is the _________.
8. The biotic communities that once lived in the Ice Age are found in the tundra and _________.
9. The treeless, low-lying, and mostly level areas found in the northern edges of Europe, Asia and North America are the _________.

10. The habitat found in two narrow strips—along the Tropic of Cancer, and the Tropic of Capricorn—is the __________ forests.

11. The evidence to show that the Sahara desert was once covered with vegetation and occupied by animals is __________.

12. The moose is found in the __________ forests.

13. __________ forests are predominantly found in Siberia.

14. The colourful climber passion flower plant is found in __________ forests.

15. The interior of __________ consists of an immense mass of ice, where nothing grows.

16. In Switzerland, there are more than __________ lakes.

17. In __________ there is an area of 250,000 square miles, known as 'The Empty Quarter' where practically no life of any kind exists.

18. Lemmings, musk ox and the polar bear are strictly __________ animals.

19. In the rocks along the river banks near __________, Baron Georges Cuvier found the bones of elephants, hippopatamuses, and many other animals no longer seen in that region.

20. The __________ is the world's richest biological ecosystem.

21. The tree, yielding a malarial drug, was once depleted from its natural habitat, and later reintroduced.

22. The major spawning areas and fish nurseries of the world are mangrove swamps and __________.

23. The primary source of food for marine animal life is __________.

24. The percentage of endemism in the 1,200 animal and plant life species recorded in Lake Baikal is __________.

25. The largest freshwater lake in the world is Lake __________.

26. The largest animal inhabiting the pampas of South America is the __________.

27. The name given to the coniferous forests in North America and Europe is __________.

28. You will find pine, spruce, redwood, fir and larch in __________ forests.

29. The only known substance that naturally exists on earth in all three chemical states is __________.

30. The tallest and thickest type of grass is the __________.

Clues

Wetlands, rain, Greenland, tropical moist forests, superior, bamboo, dodo, savannah, coniferous, Saudi Arabia, estuaries, boreal, rain forests, deer, cave paintings, 1,000, cinchona, rhea, marine, moorland, coniferous, tundra, phytoplankton, coniferous, Baikal, tundra, rain, Paris, 80, water.

45
ATMOSPHERIC FACTS

State whether the following statements about the atmosphere are true or false.

1. Atmosphere is the blanket of air that envelopes the earth.
2. The stratosphere of the atmosphere is in constant contact with the earth's surface.
3. The layer of the atmosphere which prevents the flow of the fatal ultra-violet radiation from reaching the earth is the magnetosphere.
4. The layer above the ionosphere is the magnetosphere.
5. The air surrounding the earth moves forever due to the sun's heat.
6. The sky appears blue because of the scattering of light by dust particles or air molecules in the atmosphere.
7. Only half the ultra-violet rays from the sun ever reach the earth's ground, as many are absorbed in the earth's atmosphere.
8. About 100 million grams of material enters the atmosphere each year and makes its way to the earth's sphere.
9. Hydrogen plays a decisive role in affecting the climate of the earth.
10. Supersonic aircraft and rockets cause maximum damage to the ozone layer.

11. The lithosphere, the top crust of the earth, constitutes about one per cent of its mass.
12. Fixation of atmospheric nitrogen on land is carried out by organisms called diazotrophs.
13. Climatic changes to date are in the balance of gases that form the earth's atmosphere, converting nitrogen into assimilable forms by artificial methods.
14. The World Energy Council reported in 1997 that the global emissions of carbon dioxide had increased by 2 per cent between 1990 and 1995.
15. The most dangerous hot wind 'John' that burns villages and melts snow occurs in Switzerland.

46
GEOGRAPHICAL DATA

Choose the right option to complete the sentences giving geographical data.

1. There are thermal areas in __________ where, because of the earth's crust being extremely thin, the energy bottled up below the surface bursts through in the form of boiling mud ponds.

   a. Kenya

   b. New Zealand

   c. Denver

   d. Italy

2. Magnetic north is __________ miles west of the North Pole.

a. 1,500 miles
b. 500 miles
c. 100 miles
d. 50 miles

3. The mean annual temperature in _________, just below the Arctic Circle, is higher than that in New York.
   a. Thule
   b. Murmansk
   c. Banks Island
   d. Reykjavik

4. It is possible to sail all the way round the earth on latitude _________ degrees south.
   a. 40
   b. 60
   c. 20
   d. 45

5. As the earth whirls round on its axis, a spot on the equator moves at over _________ miles per hour.
   a. 100
   b. 250
   c. 500
   d. 1,000

6. The diameter of the earth's orbit is exactly _________ times the distance that the light travels in one second.
   a. 500

b. 1,000
c. 10,000
d. 15,000

7. The midnight sun ensures that there is constant daylight for 24 hours each day for 73 consecutive days in northern __________.
   a. Finland
   b. Japan
   c. Sweden
   d. Norway

8. The deepest crater by a meteorite is in __________, and is 1,200 metres wide.
   a. Mongolia
   b. Canada
   c. Algeria
   d. Arizona

9. __________ City is sinking at the rate of 6 to 8 inches a year because it is built on top of an underground reservoir.
   a. New York
   b. Mexico
   c. Nasser
   d. Oklahoma

10. __________ is the only country that is also a continent and an island.
    a. Antarctica

b. Australia

c. Africa

d. Eurasia

11. The earth is __________ billion years old, and this fact was determined by radiometric dating that uses the decay of elements with long half-life isotopes.

    a. three

    b. three and a half

    c. four

    d. four and a half

12. __________ was the supercontinent that began to break up about 225 million years ago, eventually fragmenting into the continents as we know them today.

    a. Atlantis

    b. Micronesia

    c. Pangaea

    d. Laurasia

13. The distance from the surface of the earth to its centre is __________ miles.

    a. 3,700

    b. 2,900

    c. 4,600

    d. 1,900

14. Mt. __________ in Ecuador supports the only glacier on the equator because of temperatures that drop as low as zero degrees for extended periods.

a. Cotopaxi
b. Chimbarazo
c. Huascaran
d. Hampu

15. It takes __________ minutes for sunlight to reach the earth.
a. six
b. eight
c. nine
d. ten

16. The rotation of the earth is not felt at the __________.
a. poles
b. equator
c. tropics
d. temperate zones

17. The weight of a matter at the centre of the earth is __________.
a. five grams
b. five kilograms
c. fifty kilograms
d. zero

18. The downward movement of large masses of land, ice, earth or rock is known as an __________.
a. ice drift
b. avalanche

c. isotherm
d. isobar

19. The highest mountain in New Zealand is Mount __________, named after a famous explorer.
  a. Whakart
  b. Franklyn
  c. Cook
  d. Egmont

20. The city of __________ rests on more than 100 small islands.
  a. Venice
  b. Amsterdam
  c. Geneva
  d. Cologne

21. The highest island peak of the world, a volcano, is Mount Kea in __________.
  a. Bahamas
  b. Tasmania
  c. Hawaii
  d. Timor

22. __________ is famous for forests of cork trees.
  a. Malaysia
  b. Portugal
  c. Indonesia
  d. Ghana

23. Kamchatka Peninsula at the eastern end of _________ has 20 geysers, spurting steam and water, and over 60 active volcanoes.
   a. Vietnam
   b. South Korea
   c. Malaysia
   d. Russia

24. Over half of all the known types of flowers in the world grow in _________.
   a. Brazil
   b. South Africa
   c. Holland
   d. Indonesia

25. The most northerly town in the world is _________, where the temperature in January is a little below freezing.
   a. Hammerfest
   b. Vadso
   c. Murmansk
   d. Barrow

26. At the equinoxes in _________ and _________ there is equal number of hours of light and darkness everywhere on the earth.
   a. January, July
   b. May, October
   c. March, September
   d. June, December

27. Doubtful Sound is the name of an _________ in South Island, New Zealand.
   a. estuary
   b. island
   c. inlet
   d. isthmus

28. The trunk of the _________ tree in Kenya is so large that some natives make their homes inside the hollowed-out trunks.
   a. baobab
   b. teak
   c. peepal
   d. neem

29. On the island of _________ there is a place called the 'Valley of the Butterflies' where thousands of butterflies are attracted and are so thick that they darken the landscape.
   a. Papua New Guinea
   b. Rhodes
   c. Kiribati
   d. Pitcairn

30. There is an archipelago in South-west _________ which has 30,000 islands.
   a. Alaska
   b. California
   c. Nigeria
   d. Finland

47
WILDLIFE SANCTUARIES AND PARKS

Name the country in which the following national parks or sanctuaries are present.

1. Iguazu National Park
2. Lorentz National Park
3. Greater St. Lucia Wetland Park
4. Purnululu National Park
5. Iguacu National Park
6. Los Katios National Park
7. Sangay National Park
8. Keoladeo National Park
9. Lake Turkana National Park
10. Kinabalu Park
11. Royal Chitwan National Park
12. Manu National Park
13. Mana Pools National Park
14. Canaima National Park
15. Great Smoky Mountains National Park
16. Srebarna Nature Reserve
17. Dja Faunal Reserve
18. Okapi Wildlife Reserve
19. Rio Platano Biosphere Reserve
20. Tsingy de Bemaraha Strict Nature Reserve

21. Whale Sanctuary of El Vizcaino
22. Air and Tenere Natural Reserves
23. Arabian Oryx Sanctuary
24. Djoudj National Bird Sanctuary
25. Sinharaja Forest Reserve
26. Gough Island Wildlife Reserve
27. Selous Game Reserve
28. Angkor National Park
29. Virunga National Park
30. Wood Buffalo National Park

48
MORE ON WILDLIFE RESERVES

State whether the following interesting facts about sanctuaries and reserves are true or false.

1. Kaziranga National Park in Assam was India's first national park.
2. The main rhinoceros sanctuary of India is Baishipali.
3. The Dumkhar Sanctuary is meant to protect the sloth bear.
4. The headquarters of the World Wildlife Fund is based in Gland, Switzerland.
5. Gir Forest in Gujarat is the last home of the Indian Leopard.

6. The world's first white tiger safari was inaugurated in 1991 in Nandan Kanan, Bhubaneswar.
7. The Altos do Campana National Park in Panama is famous for a great variety of birds.
8. The Dachigam National Park in Kashmir is the last refuge of the hangul.
9. The Point Calimere sanctuary is located in the Coromandel Coast.
10. The Black River Gorge in Mauritius is the last refuge of the echo parakeet.
11. The Kusciusko National Park in Australia is famous for the rare mountain pygmy koala bear.
12. The Kirkonose National Park in Czech is included in the IUCN list of the world's most threatened protected areas on account of acid rain pollution.
13. The petrified Forest National Park in Arizona is famous for its multicoloured and millions of years old tree trunks and logs which have turned to stone.
14. The Katarniaghat Crocodile Sanctuary, known to have the largest number of gharials, is in Aurangabad.
15. The Yellowstone National Park in USA is the first designated national park in the world.
16. The Dudhwa National Park in India is famous for its large number of Swamp Deer.
17. The Jim Corbett Park in the Kumaon Hills at the foothills of the Himalayas protects the tiger.

18. The Kanha National Park in Madhya Pradesh has been described as the best place for the viewing of tigers.

19. The last home of the Northern White Rhino is in the Garamba National Park in Venezuela.

20. In 1938 the Viceroy and his party shot more than four thousand birds in one day at the Keoladeo Ghana Bird Sanctuary in Bharatpur.

21 The Kilimanjaro National Park of Janzania has the highest peak in Africa.

22. The Tsava East National Park of Kenya is famous for its Lugard Falls on River Galana.

23. The Lambwe Valley National Park in Kenya was created to protect the Roan Antelope.

24. The Kutai National Park is the last refuge of the endemic bird Bali Starling.

25. The Mapimi Reserve in Mexico protects an endangered species of tortoise with the help of local people.

26. The Little Rann of Kutch is the largest nesting site of the greater flamingo.

27. The Sagarmatha National Park in Sri Lanka was declared a world heritage site in 1979.

28. The Guatapo National Park in Venezuela protects the catchment areas of four dams.

29. The gorilla is protected in the Virunga Volcanoes National Park.

30. In the Tsavo West National Park of Kenya are the famous Mzima Springs that gush out 50 million gallons of water every day.

49
OUR SOLAR SYSTEM

Choose the right option to complete the sentences about our solar system.

1. Jupiter, Saturn, Uranus and Neptune are known as the giant __________ planets.
   a. inner
   b. outer
   c. alien
   d. ringed

2. __________ is the planet that two US Viking spacecraft landed on in 1976.
   a. Mars
   b. Venus
   c. Mercury
   d. Jupiter

3. __________ is the smallest planet.
   a. Mercury
   b. Venus
   c. Mars
   d. Pluto

4. __________ is the largest planet, and would have become a star if it had been 50 times larger to have enough density, gravity and internal heat energy to generate a thermonuclear reaction.

   a. Saturn

   b. Jupiter

   c. Uranus

   d. Neptune

5. __________ is the planet that has a moonlike crated surface, and a slight magnetic field.

   a. Mars

   b. Venus

   c. Mercury

   d. Pluto

6. __________is also known as the Evening Star because of its brightness in the sky.

   a. Mercury

   b. Venus

   c. Mars

   d. Saturn

7. The __________ uses an estimated 22 million billion tonnes of hydrogen in a year.

   a. Sun

   b. Moon

   c. Star

   d. Planet

8. Our sun is about 30,000 light years from the centre of the ________.
   a. Moon
   b. Earth
   c. Universe
   d. Milky Way

9. Gravity on the surface of the star________ is 250,000 times greater than the earth's gravity.
   a. Sirius
   b. Orion
   c. Antarres
   d. Capella

10. Up to 30,000 tonnes of ________ dust are deposited on the earth each year.
    a. red
    b. hard
    c. sandy
    d. cosmic

11. The fifth satellite of ________ was discovered only in 1948.
    a. Jupiter
    b. Saturn
    c. Uranus
    d. Neptune

12. Ninety-five per cent of the sun's matter consists of either hydrogen or ________.

a. oxygen
b. nitrogen
c. helium
d. carbon dioxide

13. A Martian year is __________ days long, compared to 365 days on earth.
    a. 687
    b. 786
    c. 678
    d. 876

14. The surface temperature of Venus is nearly __________ degrees Fahrenheit, hot enough to melt most spacecraft materials.
    a. 400
    b. 600
    c. 800
    d. 900

15. The atmosphere of Venus has clouds of__________.
    a. hydrogen
    b. icy particles
    c. sulphuric acid
    d. dust

16. When two full moons occur in any calendar month, the second full moon is called a __________ moon.
    a. white

b. blue
c. pale
d. bright

17. The planet __________ rotates in the opposite direction to the earth.
a. Venus
b. Mars
c. Jupiter
d. Uranus

18. The satellite __________ of Saturn is nicknamed the 'Death Star'.
a. Mimas
b. Europa
c. Ganymede
d. Callisto

19. Van Allen Belt is a zone of __________ in the ionosphere.
a. duest particles
b. vacuum
c. helium
d. ozone

20. The largest terrestrial planet is the __________.
a. Earth
b. Mars
c. Jupiter
d. Saturn

50
RANDOM QUIZ ON NATURE

1. Which snake has special cells between its nostrils and its eye which are sensitive to infrared radiant heat?
2. Which mosquitoes do not bite?
3. When do lunar eclipses occur?
4. What mammal is considered a dolphin despite its much greater length of 30 feet?
5. Which mineral will not dissolve in acid?
6. During midsummer, the radical leaves of which plant invariably point precisely north and south?
7. Where in the world is the origin of white tigers?
8. Which insect, when disturbed, defends itself by setting off a series of explosions, sometimes even four or five in succession?
9. Which phenomenon occurring on the surface of the sun is an optical illusion?
10. Which animal rarely mates with its close relatives despite living together?
11. Which fish is often grown in tanks and acclaimed as an excellent food?
12. Which metal, though less reactive, tarnishes when it, remains in contact with air for long?
13. Which part of the earth contains the maximum quantity of silicate minerals?

14. Which is the highest mountain in Antarctica?
15. In a really cold place which is the smallest mammal?
16. Which arachnid, contrary to belief, is timid and only bites when molested, and if hungry, the female will eat her mate?
17. Which moth has a wing span of 11 inches?
18. Haw many layers in the atmosphere divided on the basis of the distance from the surface of the earth?
19. Which volcano is considered to be sacred and is worshipped?
20. What law is concerned with the direction of planetary winds?
21. What is the size of a newly born kangaroo?
22. Which part of the sun comes into view during a total eclipse?
23. Which male moth has a keen sense of smell and can detect a female moth more than six miles away?
24. Which is the longest gulf in the world?
26. Which mammal's song, recorded deep in the ocean, ranges from deep roaring to falsetto singing?
27. Which mammals, except man and monkey, are colour blind?
28. Which insect can pull ten times its own weight?
29. Which is the largest natural lake in the world?

30. Which is the world's most remote, inhabited island?
31. What killed thousands of sheep in Texas in 1877?
32. Where can you find the world's only living prehistoric lizards that reach 10 feet in length?
33. In which continent would you find the Atlas Mountains?
34. Where would you find the Black, Red and White Volta rivers?
35. Which animal does baby-sitting for its fellow?
36. What divides Asia from North America?
37. Where is Mosquito Coast?
38. Which fern is called the Walking Fern?
39. Which plant can absorb nitrogen in the form of ammonia?
40. Which waterfalls in Norway is the highest glacier-fed falls?
41. Which volcano surrounds the Pacific Ocean plate?
42. Where is the Wulingyuan Scenic and Historic Interest Area?
43. How many deaths occurred in Calcutta when an earthquake hit it on October 11, 1737?
44. Which animal adds an additional spiral section to its horns every year?
45. Which bird with a special comb on its toes also treats its feathers on its body?

46. Which crab has legs that can span over 12 feet?

47. How many moons does Mars have?

48. Which valuable metal produces atomic power?

49. Where are the long-tailed fowls, which have tails more than 20 feet long, found?

50. Where can you find a herd of 4,000 elephants in Zimbabwe?

51. Where will you find 100,000 million stars?

52. Which animal can hop at an estimated speed of 41 km per hour?

53. Which feline animal in Ethiopia produces many perfumes in its gland?

54. Which body of water is a salty lake that is 1,300 feet below sea level, and is the lowliest spot on the surface of the earth?

55. Of what material are the shoes worn by Australian aborigines made, and which leave no tracks?

56. Which animal has 18 pairs of ribs?

57 Which is the largest living animal without a backbone?

58. Which spider is unable to spin a web?

59. Which long-eared animal of North Africa has a coat that is half wool and half hair?

60. Which nightingale sings?

61. Which animals are born on land and have to be taught how to swim by their parents?

62. Which sea animal has an eye on the end of each of its five arms?

63. Which mammal catches insects and avoids objects in its path by emitting squeaks, then listening for the echoes to return?

64. Which ducks do not appear to know how to swim?

65. Which beetle lives only a few weeks, yet its larva lives four years?

66. Which creature shields its young from the cold by hobbling along with the chick between its feet?

67. Where does most of the gold come from?

68. Which insects live in homes that are hexagonal in shape built to allow maximum space using the least amount of wax?

69. Which ounce of metal can be beaten into a sheet covering 9.3 sq. mts, or drawn into 80.5 km of wire?

70. Which bird can see 100 times better than a human being at night?

71. Which creature's egg is big enough to make a 12-man omelette?

72. Which animal's sound is the loudest among animals in the world?

73. Which is the fastest flying insect at 50 to 60 miles per hour?

74. What do Lake Powell, Lake Mead and Lake Nasser all have in common?

75. What percentage of the earth's total water supply is drinkable, fresh water?
76. What percentage of the world's fresh water is stored as glacial ice?
77. A volcanic landslide in 1792 killed more than 15,000 people, the landslide sweeping into the sea and triggering a destructive tsunami that destroyed many fishing villages. Where did this happen?
78. How many volcanoes actually form the Big Island of Hawaii?
79. Which is the fiercest animal in the world when cornered?
80. Which is the fastest flying bird in the world?
81. What do the elephant, the rhinoceros and the hippopotamus have in common?
82. Which is the only andromous fish found in India?
83. What is the special name given to cranes?
84. What is a fox's tail called?
85. Which Australian bird laughs like a human being?
86. What is a two-humped Asian camel called?
87. Which is the largest bay in the world?
88. Which is the longest strait?
89. Name the largest peninsula in the world.
90. Which is the greatest plateau in the world?

91. Which is the widest waterfall that is nearly seven miles wide?
92. Name the highest lake in the world.
93. On which river is Washington situated?
94. Which tree yields natural chewing gum?
95. Which plant's flower yields the saffron of commerce?
96. Which is the largest cactus in the world?
97. Which oldest known living seed was found in frozen silt in Canada in 1954, its estimated age being 10,000 years?
98. Which country has the maximum number of orchids in the world?
99. Which tree yields the heaviest wood in the world?
100. Which is the tallest palm in the world?
101. Which is the oldest tree alive today?
102. Which animals use an ultrasonic sonar to detect their prey?
103. Of all the domestic animals which is the only one that does not live in social groups?
104. How many teeth does a turtle have, as it can deliver a nasty bite?
105. Which river runs through Kashmir?
106. What is the hippopotamus also known as?
107. What is the snake-bird commonly known as?

108. Where would you find the black-necked crane in India?

109. This metal does not rust, is useful in making pipes, tanks and boilers, and mixed with tin, becomes bronze. Which is it?

110. Name the river which flows through Rome.

111. Which active Italian volcano erupted in the 1970's and 1980's?

112. Which animal's teeth were used for dentures many years ago, as they did not turn yellow?

113. Which animal, believed to have been extinct, was discovered existing along a narrow foothill belt in Assam?

114. Which is the most massive tree in the world?

115. Which is the tallest recorded bamboo in the world?

116. Which butterfly disappeared from its former range of occurrence due to wetland drainage?

117. What is a katydid?

118. On which river is the city of Lucknow situated?

119. Name a living fossil tree considered to have become extinct 20 million years ago, which was discovered in 1941 in China.

120. Name the plant producing the largest inflorescence in the world.

121. How many species of deer are found in Africa?

122. What is the base of the bill in birds sometimes covered by a peculiar type of skin?

123. What is the preferred habbit of the green python?

124. To which group do salamanders belong?

125. To which group of animals do sharks belong?

126. What is the chemical nature of the spider web?

127. Where is the wildlife Institute of India located?

128. What is the name given to the death of a plant or animal without reproduction, and irretrievable loss of populations?

129. Name a national park in Kenya famous for perpetual snow on the equator of the earth.

130. Which city in India is situated at the confluence of the Ganges and the Yamuna?

131. From which language is the word 'Planet' derived?

132. What do you call the revolution of the solar system around the centre of the Milky Way?

133. What is the innermost layer in the sun called?

134. Which dog in South Africa once hunted lions?

135. Which tree, considered to have become extinct a few hundred years ago, are now being supported in Darjeeling and Almora?

136. What is a type of zebra striped on the head, neck and shoulders, and is now extinct, called?

137. Which male animal inflates its nose till it becomes like a large balloon, when it is angry?

138. Which fish feeds on lotus leaves, skinned bananas, boiled rice, tomatoes and weeds that may be found in garbage filled and weed-infested ponds?

139. Which female mammal has the largest litters?

140. The oil of which fish is used in the oiling of precision equipment?

141. Which is the planet with the lowest gravitational pull?

142. What are asteroids also called?

143. What is 99 per cent of the crust of the earth composed?

144. Which volcano in Japan, after remaining dormant for two years, erupted on 31 March 2000?

145. What is caused when warm air is surrounded by cold air?

146. Which river flows through a plain of yellow sand, and during a storm, gets deposited with the yellow sand?

147. Where in the USA is the Yellowstone National Park?

148. Which is the smallest nation in Africa?

149. Where is the world's largest seaport?

150. Where is the world's highest navigable lake?

151. How many eyelids do camels have to protect themselves from blowing sand?

152. Which octopus grows from the size of a pea to a 68 kg behemoth, potentially 30 feet across, in just two years?

153. What is common among the humming bird, loon, swift, kingfisher and grebe?

154. Located on the islands off the coast of which country is the largest bird colony in the world?

155. To which country can the origin of coffee be traced?

156. Which is the hardest of all the world's insects?

157. How many years does it take for an oyster to produce a medium-sized pearl?

158. Which flower releases a chemical that makes bees drunk?

159. Which plant cannot reproduce itself, but has to be propagated by man?

160. Which river divided Paraguay into its two distinct halves?

161. Which territory is the southernmost part of Europe?

162. Where in the world is the Great Barrier Reef found?

163. Which planet is known as the red planet?

164. Which is the longest waterfall in Asia?

165. Which is the rainiest place in the world?

166. In which continent did the tomato originate?

167. To which family do potatoes, eggplants, peppers and tobacco belong?

168. What is the coffee grown in Brazil called?

169. Where do the finest emeralds come from?

170. Where was the "Welcome Stranger" gold nugget, weighing 70 kgs, found?

171. Where did the watermelon originate?

172. Where would you find the Garden of Gethsemane where some olive trees have been alive for two thousand years?

173. How old are the cave drawings of animals in southern France and Spain?

174. What are the reptiles that lived 230 million years ago in the Age of Reptiles called?

175. What is a narwhal that has a long ivory tusk on the left side of its mouth that sticks out in front like a sword?

176. Where are sea otters found in streams and lakes?

177. Which are the smallest living animals with a backbone?

178. What is the other name for the rainbow fish?

179. Which is the smallest anteater that lives in the area between southern Mexico and Brazil?

180. What is the duckbill also known as?

181. How long does the sun shine in Antarctica in winter?

182. Which is the oldest known plant?

183. Which is the smallest flowering plant?

184. Where did the flower dahlia originate?

185. Which flower, a native of South America, is also known by the name of Marvel of Peru?

186. Which is the national flower of India?

187. To which family of plants does the lady's slipper belong?

188. What type of marking do yellow flowers have to attract bees and butterflies?

189. What are forest areas with very cold winters classed as?

190. How many years ago did the Jurassic forest exist?

191. What type of forest first existed on this earth?

192. The giant leaf measuring 1.8 metres of which plant is found in South America?

193. To which group do fleshy fruits with a hard stone inside or a single seed belong?

194. How many stars are bright and visible without a telescope?

195. Which bee bores a tunnel with several cells through wood and leaves, and then lays an egg in each cell?

196. Which cat, measuring about 1.2 metres long, including its tail, is found in Australian forests?

197. Which monkey, although named 'ape' is not an ape, yet it has no tail and is the only wild monkey living in Europe?

198. What neutron regularly sends radio waves?

199. Name the bee that builds its nest on a stone wall.

200. What are falling stars or glowing stars otherwise known as?

201. Which African tree, bearing a fruit called the monkey bread, can live for almost a thousand years?

202. How many varieties of bats are there in the world?

203. How do orchids reproduce?

204. Which is the shallowest ocean with an average depth of 3,580 metres?

205. Which is the only poisonous snake found in Britain?

206. Which plant snaps open its bladder to trap a mosquito?

207. Which brilliant constellation includes two of the brightest stars?

208. Which birds are known as the brain fever birds of Africa?

209. Which tree in India is considered sacred as Buddha achieved enlightenment under its shade?

210. Besides chlorine, sodium, sulphur and magnesium, which are the other two elements responsible for the saltiness of sea water?

211. What is the fertile area in a desert called?

212. Which bird builds an oven like a clay nest?

213. What is a flying fish?

214. What rare animal is protected in Hsifan Park in China?

215. Which Malayan monkey with an arm spread of about two metres has become an engendered species?

216. Which tall, pointed trees with fan-like leaves have remain unchanged for over a million years?

217. What is a small kangaroo called?

218. Which river in Africa has the largest delta?

219. Which bird follows in the wake of a ship for long distances?

220. Which is the biggest species of owls in the world?

221. Which noisy bird of Australia was rediscovered in 1961 after its long believed extinction from 1889?

222. Which Indian emperor formulated laws for wildlife preservation?

223. By what name are the coniferous forests known in major parts of Asia?

224. Which plants yields the golden fruit of the Andes?

225. Which is the most delicious fruit in the world?

226. Which is the most beautiful of all flowering trees in the world?

227. Which fungus is used in the fermentation of alcohol?

228. Name the American plant with a flower strike partly arched over by a hood-like covering.

229. Which conifer is grown all over the world for its timber and for making paper?

230. If a species of plant contains selenium, what does the soil in which it has grown certainly contain?

231. What constitutes a major part of Antarctic vegetation?

232. Which desert is often frequented by joy-riders, leading to the extinction of its flora and fauna?

233. Where is the Valley of Flowers in India located?

234. Which are the most successful and widespread of all land plants?

235. Which shrub, brought from Australia to decorate garden hedges in India, has become a weed?

236. What were those native grains that Columbus brought from Cuba to Europe, where they were cultivated and then distributed to the entire world?

237. From where was eucalyptus brought to Europe?

238. Cocoa is the native of which continent?

239. Which plant is known as the gasoline plant?

240. From the leaves of which plant native to Egypt is a laxative obtained?

241. What are plants and animals living at the bottom of a sea or lake called?

242. What is known as a mineral crop?

243. Which is the most successful and evolving mammal of the animal kingdom?

244. Which is the animal that never drinks water?

245. Which is the rarest marsupial?

246. Which is the largest rodent in the world?

247. Which animal's skin is called the Hudson Seal by furriers?

248. Which animal defends itself by squirting an obnoxious liquid called mercaptan?

249. Which animal has the thickest skin among animals?

250. Name the South American animal which is like a camel but is short-statured.

ANSWERS

1. BLOOMS AND BLOSSOMS

1. acacia
2. anemone
3. anthurium
4. antirrhinum
5. aster
6. chrysanthemum
7. dahlia
8. daisy
9. delphinum
10. foxglove
11. freesia
12. gladiolus
13. hyacinth
14. lilac
15. lupine
16. marigold
17. orchid
18. peony
19. phlox
20. tulip
21. gerbera
22. pansy
23. carnation
24. hollyhock
25. buttercup

2. SAY IT WITH FLOWERS

1. True
2. True
3. True
4. False - It was Holland
5. False - It is in Malaysia
6. True
7. False - It is nasturtium
8. True
9. True
10. True
11. False
12. True
13. True
14. True
15. False - Tuberose is called so.
16. True
17. False - It is *Protea repeans*
18. True
19. True
20. False - They are pink and yellow
21. True
22. True
23. False - They have long stamens
24. False
25. True

3. FLOWERY EMBLEMS

1. b
2. g
3. k
4. f
5. j
6. d
7. a
8. o
9. c
10. m
11. e
12. n
13. h
14. l
15. i
16. t
17. p
18. s
19. q
20. r

4. A GARDEN OF FLOWERS

1. Azalea
2. Balsam
3. Cosmos
4. Daffodil
5. Honeysuckle
6. Begonia
7. Hibiscus
8. Canna
9. Chrysanthemum
10. Violet
11. Cornflower
12. Snapdragon
13. Petunia
14. Sweetpea
15. Larkspur
16. Sunflower
17. Peony
18. Pansy
19. Carnation
20. Primrose
21. Buttercup
22. Daisy
23. Crocus
24. Snowdrop
25. Geranium

5. WHAT FLOWER AM I?

1. Marigold
2. Amaryllis
3. Morning Glory
4. Climatis

6. QUALITY FLOWERS

1. 10
2. 18
3. 24
4. 4
5. 16
6. 1
7. 20
8. 6
9. 2
10. 17
11. 8
12. 13
13. 3
14. 15
15. 7
16. 22
17. 5
18. 25
19. 12
20. 23
21. 9
22. 14
23. 11
24. 27
25. 19
26. 30
27. 21
28. 29
29. 28
30. 26

7. HANDSOME FOLIAGE

1. True
2. True
3. False - *Erythroxylum cocoa*
4. False - contain sweet enzyme
5. True
6. True
7. True
8. True
9. True
10. True
11. False
12. True
13. False - north and south

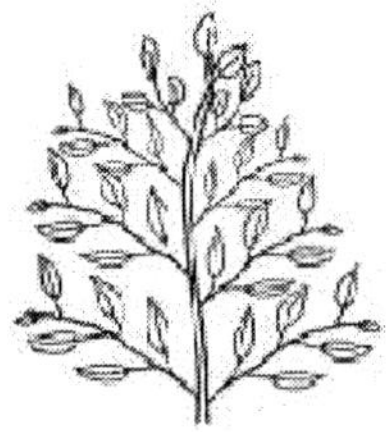

14. False
15. True
16. True
17. False - needle-like leaves
18. True
19. False
20. True
21. True
22. False - from a leaf bud
23. True
24. True
25. False

8. NUTCRACKERS

1. Almond
2. Betelnut
3. Brazilnut
4. Cashew
5. Coconut
6. Acorn
7. Pistachio
8. Kolanut
9. Nutmeg
10. Pecan
11. Hazelnut
12. Peanut
13. Chestnut
14. Walnut
15. Arecanut
16. Hickory

9. FRUITY FLAVOURS

1. Apple
2. Pineapple
3. Pear
4. Orange
5. Banana
6. Lime
7. Lemon
8. Grape
9. Plum
10. Papaya
11. Mango
12. Litchi
13. Apricot
14. Peach
15. Olive
16. Melon
17. Pomegranate
18. Guava
19. Watermelon
20. Cherry

10. NATURE'S BOUNTEOUS TREES

1. angle
2. redwood
3. squirrels
4. 100
5. bark
6. four
7. cinchona
8. ornamental
9. conifers
10. jelly
11. flowering
12. acacia
13. conifer
14. ash
15. larch
16. tamarind
17. gulmohar
18. beech
19. chestnut
20. sycamore
21. willow
22. pine

11. WOODY FORESTS

1. maple
2. sapling
3. rings
4. three
5. Brazil
6. rainforest
7. autecology
8. Australia
9. eucalyptus
10. trees
11. neem
12. mountain
13. savannas
14. Jurassic
15. Andamans
16. four
17. gum
18. coniferous
19. temperate
20. grass

12. HERBAL FARE

1. dill
2. cassia
3. cardamom
4. asafoetida
5. basil
6. liquorice
7. margosa
8. nutmeg
9. rosemary
10. sage
11. aniseed
12. spearmint
13. peppermint
14. caraway
15. thyme
16. lavender
17. fenugreek
18. cineraria
19. vanilla
20. calendula
21. saffron
22. fennel
23. ginseng
24. marjoram
25. cuminseed
26. parsley
27. castor
28. pepper
29. chamomile
30. clove

13. FOUR-FOOTED ANIMALS

1. lions
2. tiger
3. white
4. snow
5. cheetah
6. jungle
7. lynx
8. caracal
9. civet
10. hyena
11. wolf
12. jackal
13. foxes
14. mongoose
15. otter
16. sloth
17. panda
18. elephant
19. rhinoceros
20. yak

21. gaur
22. urial
23. antelope
24. buck
25. stags
26. musk
27. hanuman
28. zebra
29. horn
30. bone

14. MONKEY BUSINESS

1. Pygmy Marmoset
2. Mandrell
3. Man of the woods
4. Long-tailed
5. Red-capped Mangabey
6. Gorilla
7. 1986
8. Aye-aye
9. Gorilla
10. Three
11. Herbivorous
12. Gorilla
13. Japanese Macaque
14. Borneo
15. Lemur
16. Orang-utan
17. Chimpanzee
18. Mountain Gorilla
19. Gorillas
20. Flying Lemur
21. Large leaves
22. Orang-utan
23. Mountain forest of Assam
24. Siamang Gibbon
25. Hanuman Langur

15. DOG MUDDLE

1. Greyhound
2. Cocker spaniel
3. Collie
4. Dalmatian
5. Pekinese
6. Alsatian
7. Poodle
8. Labrador

9. Bulldog
10. Dachshund
11. Red setter
12. Scotch terrier
13. German shepherd
14. Boxer
15. Irish setter

16. THE DOG FAMILY

1. True
2. False - through their paws
3. True
4. True
5. False - it is a squirrel rodent
6. True
7. False - it is Airedale Terrier
8. True
9. True
10. False

17. FELINE GRACE

1. lynx
2. cat
3. manx
4. cheetah
5. panthers
6. ragdoll
7. lion
8. civet
9. tigress
10. black-footed
11. cougar
12. pugmark
13. leopard
14. India
15. leopard
16. 284
17. Siberia
18. Jaguar
19. *Akbarnama*
20. Margay

18. YOUNG ONES

1. 7
2. 5
3. 1
4. 8
5. 10
6. 12
7. 3
8. 13
9. 14
10. 21
11. 24
12. 2
13. 9
14. 4
15. 6
16. 18
17. 11
18. 15
19. 23
20. 22
21. 20
22. 17
23. 25
24. 19
25. 16
26. 30
27. 26
28. 29
29. 27
30. 28

19. HOME SWEET HOME

1. sty
2. dry
3. hutch
4. cavities
5. ground
6. tunnel
7. mud
8. tailor
9. kennel
10. stable
11. lyre
12. dovecot
13. burrow
14. den
15. lair

20. MAMMALIAN ANIMALS

1. Bandicoot - a rodent
2. Lemur - only higher mammal to be airborne
3. Poodle - not a hound
4. Yak - only animal suited for desert and mountain climates.
5. Gaur - not a wild ass
6. Zebu - main species of cattle roaming on Indian streets.
7. Armadillo - not an odd-toed unguate
8. Dingo - not a cat family member
9. Dhole - not a deer family
10. Lynx - it is a baby-lifter
11. Dhole - hunts its prey in a pack
12. Ibex - lives at great altitudes near the snowline
13. Musk deer - has no antlers and has tusk-like incisors
14. Chausingha - only antelope in the world with two pairs of horns
15. Llama - the only vegetarian

21. FEATHERED FRIENDS

1. wren
2. kagu
3. Arctic tern
4. goose
5. heron
6. ibis
7. Emperor Penguin
8. cranes
9. barn owl
10. secretary bird
11. humming bird
12. Great Blue Heron
13. kiwi
14. ostrich
15. crow
16. flamingo
17. pigeon
18. hornbill
19. Sarus Crane
20. stork
21. albatross
22. swift
23. shearwater
24. petral
25. shoebill
26. screamers
27. Golden Eagle
28. kiwi
29. secretary bird
30. Lapwing

22. MUDDLED BIRDS

1. woodpecker
2. lapwing
3. skylark
4. swallow
5. partridge
6. Arctic tern
7. secretary bird
8. road runner
9. kookaburra
10. vulture
11. cardinal
12. oriole
13. nightingale
14. macaw
15. warbler
16. goldfinch
17. robin
18. avocet
19. hornbill
20. chickadees
21. jacana
22. monal
23. hobby
24. shoebill
25. eagle
26. dove
27. penguin
28. ostrich
29. humming bird
30. falcon

23. BUTTERFLIES AND MOTHS

1. True
2. True
3. False – Birdwing Butterfly
4. False – Atlas Moth
5. False – Milkweed

6. True
7. True
8. True
9. False – it is the Monarch Butterfly
10. True
11. True
12. False – they are butterflies
13. False – they are moths
14. True
15. True

Queen Alexandra's birdwing butterfly

24. INSECT LIFE

1. frog
2. wasp
3. wingless
4. beetles
5. cockroaches
6. cicada
7. snail
8. flea
9. dragonfly
10. swallowtail

11. Goliath
12. fly
13. Tumblebug
14. Giant African Snail
15. honey
16. six
17. stag
18. cricket
19. fleas
20. garbage
21. cockroach
22. ants
23. locusts
24. sound
25. greenbottle
26. silverfish
27. headlice
28. bugs
29. dragonflies
30. termite

25. CREEPY CRAWLIES

1. teeth
2. python
3. 200
4. chameleon
5. crocodiles
6. lizard
7. python
8. grass
9. tortoises
10. anaconda
11. boa constrictor
12. sea snake
13. lizard
14. iguana
15. alligator
16. estuarine
17. gharial
18. turtle
19. vegetation
20. leatherback

26. THE AMPHIBIANS

1. True
2. True
3. True
4. True
5. True
6. False - because it never grows up
7. True
8. False - they are used in Chinese medicine
9. False - it is the Arrow-poison frog
10. True

11. False – it is the Texas Blind Salamander
12. False – by gliding
13. True
14. False – a tadpole has no neck
15. False

27. MOLLUSCS

1. oyster
2. clam
3. octopus
4. mussel
5. snail
6. squid
7. cuttlefish
8. slug

28. FISHY TALES

1. deep sea angler
2. paradise fish
3. archer fish
4. trident fish
5. paddlefish
6. codfish
7. candlefish
8. angler
9. man-eater
10. angler
11. sucker
12. electric eel
13. Physalia jellyfish
14. cuttlefish
15. barracuda
16. flying fish
17. lung fish
18. stickle back fish
19. elephant fishes
20. Philippino dwarf pygmy
21. sunfish
22. Beluga sturgeon
23. archer fish
24. great white shark
25. sword fish
26. red bat fish
27. lake sturgeon
28. guitar fish
29. kurtur
30. catfish
31. shark
32. shark
33. catfish
34. shark
35. goldfish
36. mackerel
37. turbot fish
38. goldfish
39. parrotfish
40. climbing perchfish
41. scorpionfish
42. butterfly fish
43. mosquito fish
44. hagfish
45. bitterling fish
46. halibut
47. sucker fish
48. pomfret
49. mudskipper
50. doctor fish

Butterfly fish

29. MARINE LIFE

1. True
2. True
3. True
4. False – it is the dolphin
5. True
6. True
7. True
8. False – they are used to dip up shellfish from the seabed.
9. True
10. True
11. True
12. True

13. False – they are animals
14. False - a dogfish is a shark
15. True
16. True
17. False – there are about 2,000 species
18. False – it takes seven years
19. True
20. False – it is the sea otter.
21. True
22. True
23. True
24. True
25. True

30. GROUPS OF ANIMALS

1. colony
2. swarm
3. army
4. plague
5. shoal
6. school
7. snock
8. hover
9. jam
10. peep
11. murder
12. dule
13. gaggle
14. brood
15. deceit
16. exaltation
17. watch
18. parliament
19. covery
20. ostentation
21. unkindness
22. building
23. host
24. mustering
25. murmuration
26. flight
27. rafter
28. descent
29. whisp
30. shrewdness
31. cete
32. sloth
33. clowder
34. drove
35. shulk
36. husk
37. cast
38. siege
39. harass
40. kindle
41. leap
42. pride
43. team
44. string
45. bitter
46. nest
47. crash
48. pod
49. flock
50. dray
51. knot
52. pitying
53. bate
54. whisp

31. PLACID LAKES

1. 5	6. 3	11. 2
2. 7	7. 14	12. 9
3. 1	8. 12	13. 4
4. 8	9. 13	14. 10
5. 11	10. 15	15. 6

32. GUSHING RIVERS

1. Nile	11. Thames	21. Niger
2. Hwangho	12. Russia	22. Darling
3. Spree	13. Amazon	23. Indus
4. Volga	14. Danube	24. Padma
5. Gangotri	15. Hudson	25. Seine
6. Shanghai	16. Shannon	26. Jordan
7. Po	17. Zambezi	27. Niagara
8. Pearl river	18. Rio Grande	28. Boyne
9. Varanasi	19. Colorado	29. Yalu
10. Brahmaputra	20. Mackenzie	30. Ob

33. SALTY SEAS

1. True
2. False – between Jordan and Israel
3. False – it is the South China Sea
4. True
5. True
6. True
7. False – enclosed by the Siberian Mainland, Kamchatka, the Kurils and Sakhalin Islands.
8. False – it is known as Huang Hai
9. True
10. True
11. True

12. True

13. False - it reflects the colour of the sky

14. True

15. True

34. DEEP OCEANS

1. Pacific
2. Arctic
3. Indian
4. Indian
5. Arctic
6. Antarctic
7. Pacific
8. Pacific
9. Kea
10. *Trieste*
11. Atlantic
12. Bermuda Triangle
13. Atlantis
14. El Nino
15. Atlantic
16. White horses
17. Java
18. Fathometer
19. 97
20. Antarctic Convergence
21. Current
22. Indian
23. Ice
24. Saltiest
25. Gulf Stream
26. Countercurrents
27. Gulf Stream
28. echo
29. high seas
30. ninth

35. CASCADING FALLS

1. Angel Falls
2. Australia
3. Norway
4. South Africa
5. Venezuela
6. New Zealand
7. California
8. Guyana
9. Cascades
10. Plunge
11. British Colombia
12. Cataract
13. Goat
14. Faults
15. Switzerland
16. Karnataka
17. France
18. Austria
19. Niagara
20. Guyana

36. BARREN DESERTS

1. True
2. False - it is one-third
3. False - less than 100 mm
4. False - it is 20 per cent
5. False - it is Australia
6. True
7. True
8. True
9. False - 1,200 species
10. True

11. False - in Israel
12. True
13. False - it is in California
14. True
15. True
16. False - between Orange and Zambezi
17. True
18. True
19. False - it is in the United States
20. False - it is in China

37. THE PEAKS

1. Nepal
2. India
3. India
4. Nepal
5. Nepal-Tibet
6. Nepal
7. India
8. Nepal
9. Alaska
10. Nepal-Tibet
11. India
12. Pakistan
13. East Africa
14. Israel
15. Alaska
16. Switzerland
17. Armenia
18. Greece
19. Italy-France
20. Switzerland

38. THE HIGHLANDS

1. Jungfrau
2. Pyrenees
3. fold
4. France
5. Fujiyama
6. residual
7. Trans-Antarctican
8. Italy
9. Scotland
10. Carpathian
11. Iceland
12. Caucasus
13. Monte Rosa
14. Spain
15. Italy
16. Greece
17. Krishna
18. Mt. Hood
19. Mt. Ararat
20. Ararat

39. STEAMY VOLCANOES

1. 5
2. 7
3. 2
4. 12
5. 6
6. 1
7. 10
8. 3
9. 15
10. 8
11. 4
12. 9
13. 11
14. 13
15. 19
16. 14
17. 20
18. 17
19. 16
20. 18

40. THE QUAKES

1. Pierre
2. Tectonic
3. Richter
4. Seismic
5. Mercalli
6. China
7. epicenter
8. manmade
9. focus
10. intermediate
11. seismic
12. R.D. Oldham
13. Lisbon
14. Mauna Loa
15. 50
16. tsunami
17. San Francisco
18. Tokyo
19. China

41. LUSTROUS METALS

1. True
2. True
3. False - cast iron is the best
4. False - it becomes reddish brown
5. True
6. True
7. True
8. True
9. False - in the form of crystals
10. True

42. HOMOGENEOUS MINERALS

1. copper
2. lead
3. copper
4. iron
5. manganese
6. bronze
7. silver
8. platinum
9. uranium
10. aluminium

These are all metals

43. AN AMALGAMATION OF METALS-MINERALS

1. aluminium
2. pyrite
3. molybdenum
4. haematite
5. titanium
6. kimberlite
7. bronze
8. gypsum

9. Witwatersrand, S.A.
10. corundum
11. India
12. calcite
13. mercury
14. magnetite
15. zinc, tin, copper
16. slate
17. nickel
18. garnet
19. copper
20. oolite
21. iron
22. polymetallic modules
23. copper

44. OUR ECOSYSTEM

1. Rain forests
2. Marine
3. Dodo
4. Baikal
5. Wetlands
6. Deer
7. Savannah
8. Moorland
9. Tundra
10. Rain
11. Cave paintings
12. Coniferous
13. Rain
14. Greenland
15. 1,000
16. Saudi Arabia
17. Tundra
18. Paris
19. Tropical moist forests
20. Cinchona
21. Estuaries
22. Phytoplankton
23. 80
24. Superior
25. Rhea
26. Boreal
27. Coniferous
28. Water
29. Bamboo

45. ATMOSPHERIC FACTS

1. True
2. False - it is troposphere
3. False - it is ionosphere
4. True
5. True
6. True
7. True
8. False - it is 1,000 million grams
9. False - it is carbon dioxide that affects
10. True
11. True
12. True
13. True
14. False - increased by 12 per cent

46. GEOGRAPHICAL DATA

1. New Zealand
2. 1,500 miles
3. Reykjavik
4. 60
5. 1,000
6. 1,000
7. Finland
8. Arizona
9. Mexico
10. Australia
11. Four and a half
12. Pangaea
13. 3,700
14. Cotopaxi
15. eight
16. poles
17. zero
18. avalanche
19. cook
20. Venice
21. Hawaii
22. Portugal
23. Russia
24. South Africa
25. Hammerfest
26. March, September
27. Inlet
28. Baobab
29. Rhodes
30. Finland

47. WILDLIFE SANCTUARIES AND PARKS

1. Argentina
2. Indonesia
3. South Africa
4. Australia
5. Brazil
6. Colombia
7. Euador
8. India
9. Kenya
10. Malaysia
11. Nepal
12. Peru
13. Zimbabwe
14. Venezuela
15. USA
16. Bulgaria
17. Cameroon
18. Congo
19. Honduras
20. Madagascar
21. Mexico
22. Niger
23. Oman
24. Senegal
25. Sri Lanka
26. UK
27. Tanzania
28. Cambodia
29. Zaire
30. Canada

48. MORE ON WILDLIFE RESERVES

1. True
2. False - it is Kaziranga, Assam
3. True
4. True
5. False - it is Asiatic Lion
6. True
7. False - variety of plants
8. True
9. True
10. True
11. False - famous for the possum
12. True
13. True
14. False - it is in Bahraich
15. True
16. True

17. True
18. True
19. False – the Park is in Zaire
20. True
21. True
22. True
23. True
24. False – it is Kutai National Park
25. True
26. False – It is Great Rann of Kutch
27. False – the park is in Nepal
28. True
29. True
30. True

49. OUR SOLAR SYSTEM

1. Outer
2. Mars
3. Pluto
4. Jupiter
5. Mars
6. Venus
7. Sun
8. Milky Way
9. Sirius
10. Cosmic
11. Uranus
12. Helium
13. 687
14. 900
15. Sulphuric acid
16. Blue
17. Uranus
18. Mimas
19. Ozone
20. Earth

50. RANDOM QUIZ ON NATURE

1. Rattlesnake
2. Male
3. During full moon
4. Killer whale
5. diamond
6. compass plant
7. India
8. bombardier beetle
9. sunspots
10. prairie dog
11. milkfish
12. silver
13. crust
14. Vinson Massif
15. fox
16. black spider widow
17. Indian Atlas Moth
18. Six
19. Mount Fujiyama
20. Ferrels Law
21. 2.5 cm
22. Corona
23. Silkworm
24. Gulf of Mexico

25. Spree
26. whale
27. all
28. earthworm
29. Caspian
30. Tristan da Cunha
31. ice bombardment
32. Komodo Island, Indonesia
33. Africa
34. Burkina Faso
35. Grey Meerkat
36. Bering Strait
37. Nicaragua
38. Adiantum
39. Paddy
40. Utigord
41. Ring of Fire
42. China
43. 300,000
44. ram
45. heron
46. Japanese spider crab
47. two
48. uranium
49. Kochi, Japan
50. Wankie National Park
51. Milky Way
52. Kangaroo
53. civet
54. Dead Sea
55. emu feathers
56. horse
57. giant squid
58. tarantula
59. sheep
60. cock
61. seals
62. starfish
63. bat
64. new-born
65. Lucanus Cervus
66. emperor penguin
67. South Africa
68. bees
69. gold
70. barn owl
71. ostrich
72. blue whale
73. dragonfly
74. all man-made lakes
75. three
76. 70
77. Japan
78. five
79. common shrew
80. swift
81. they are all pachyderms
82. hilsa
83. Daddy-long-legs
84. brush
85. kookaburra
86. bactrian camel
87. Hudson Bay
88. Tartar Strait
89. Arabia
90. Tibetan Plateau

91. Khone falls
92. Lago Titicaca
93. Potamac
94. Chile Tree
95. *Crocus sativus*
96. Saguaro
97. Arctic Lupin
98. Colombia
99. Black Iron Wood
100. Wax Palm
101. Bristle cone pine
102. Bats
103. dog
104. none
105. Jhelum
106. river horse
107. darter
108. Ladakh
109. copper
110. Tiber
111. Mt Etna
112. hippopotamus
113. Pigmy Hog
114. Giant Sequaia
115. Thorny Bamboo
116. Swallowtail
117. insect
118. Gomati
119. Dawn Redwood
120. Talipot Palm
121. four
122. cere
123. rain forests
124. amphibia
125. fish
126. protein
127. Dehradun
128. gene erosion
129. Mt Kenya National Park
130. Allahabad
131. Greek
132. cosmic year
133. photosphere
134. Rhodesian Ridgeback
135. Dawn Redwood
136. quagga
137. Elephant seal
138. Giant Gourmani
139. Common Tenrec
140. ratfish
141. Mercury
142. planetoids
143. elements
144. Mt Usu
145. cyclone
146. Hwangho or Yellow River
147. Wyoming
148. Gambia
149. Singapore
150. Bolivia
151. three
152. Pacific Giant Octopus
153. they cannot walk
154. Peru
155. East Africa
156. mosquito

157. five
158. orchid
159. banana
160. Paraguay
161. Crete
162. Australia
163. Mars
164. Gerosoppa Falls in India
165. Mount Waialeale, Hawaii
166. South America
167. Nightshade
168. Brazils
169. Bogota, Colombia
170. Australia
171. tropical Africa
172. Mount of Oliver
173. from 30,000 to 10,000 BC old
174. brontosaurus
175. a type of whale
176. from Mexico to Alaska
177. *Pandaka pygmaea* fish
178. *guppy*
179. silky
180. platypus
181. 24 hours
182. algae
183. Wolffia angasta
184. Mexico
185. Four o'clock flower
186. lotus
187. orchid
188. ultra-violet ray markings
189. Boreal forests
190. 200 million years ago
191. carboniferous forest
192. water lily
193. drupes
194. 6,000
195. carpenter bee
196. Dasyure Tiger Cat
197. barbary ape
198. pulsar
199. mason bee
200. meteors
201. baobab
202. 900
203. by cross pollination
204. Atlantic
205. adder
206. bladderwort plant
207. Orion
208. barbets
209. peepal
210. calcium and potassium
211. oasis
212. oven bird
213. a species of bat
214. Giant Panda
215. orang-utan
216. Gingko tree
217. wallaby
218. Niger
219. albatross
220. great grey owl
221. scrub bird
222. Ashoka

223. taiga
224. Naranjilla
225. durian
226. Flame Amherstia
227. fungus
228. jack-in-the pulpit
229. Silka spruce
230. uranium
231. lichens
232. California
233. Garhwal region
234. grasses
235. lantana
236. maize
237. Australia
238. South America
239. Euphorbia lathyris
240. Senna
241. benthos
242. soyabean
243. mouse
244. kangaroo rat
245. Tasmanian wolf
246. capybara
247. muskrat
248. skunk
249. whale shark
250. llama